Worcestershire Ghosts and Hauntings

To
Netty

Hope you sleep at nights!

Ann Bradford

13/8/17

Head from Beoley font circa 1140.

Worcestershire Ghosts and Hauntings

Anne Bradford

Edited by Barrie Roberts
Book design by John Bradford

BREWIN BOOKS

First published in Great Britain
by Hunt End Books 2001

This edition published by
Brewin Books Ltd, 56 Alcester Road,
Studley, Warwickshire B80 7LG in 2017
www.brewinbooks.com

ISBN: 978-1-85858-568-0

A Cataloguing in Publication Record
for this title is available from the British Library

Printed in Great Britain by
Berforts Ltd.

Acknowledgements and Introduction

This is my eighth collection of ghost stories, three of which have been co-authored with Barrie Roberts, a former criminal lawyer who specialised in the analysis of evidence and is now a writer, lecturer and consultant on the paranormal.

As usual, I have not offered any explanation to these stories and made no comment, leaving the reader to draw his or her own conclusions. I would, however, mention that telepathy has been proved under laboratory conditions, and in those rare cases where a person is thought to have transmitted a telepathic image of himself or herself, this is sometimes said to have been surrounded by a glow or aura. Poltergeist activity seems to be very common, usually manifesting itself by phantom footsteps but it does seem to include other strange noises, as well as electrical problems, difficulties with water, inanimate articles moving and so on. It usually seems to centre round a teenager, often a young female, sometimes ill or under stress. No scientific explanation has been established, though this may be due to the notorious unwillingness of scientists to venture into the paranormal. Nevertheless, some worthwhile research does get done, and vague outlines of explanations are being sketched in, mostly in the field of electro-magnetic effects on the human brain, an area which may yet yield astonishing breakthroughs.

People ask me how I manage to collect so many stories. I lecture on Ghosts, Murders and Scandals and have given talks to a variety of organisations ranging from those on Remand at Hewell Grange to Round Table Associations, and at these lectures I ask if anyone has a ghost story. I am also grateful to the local radio stations and the press for their publicity, which has resulted in many people getting in touch.

If anyone has a story, no matter how trivial, I would love to hear it. My telephone number is 01527 542516. Anonymity is guaranteed if requested. I have a habit of losing telephone numbers so if I have promised to ring you and have not done so, please get in touch with me.

The following have been especially helpful: *Redditch Standard, Bromsgrove Messenger, Evesham Journal, Malvern Gazette, Kidderminster Shuttle, Kidderminster Express and Star, Berrows Worcester Journal, Droitwich Advertiser, Hereford and Worcester Radio, ACE Radio, Redditch Advertiser, Worcester Evening Mail* and *the Birmingham Evening Mail*. I would also like to thank Tim Merridew, Alan Foxall, the staff of the Evesham Museum and Almonry and the librarians at Redditch, Evesham, Kidderminster and Bromsgrove who do their best to comply with my strange requests.

CONTENTS

Worcester Cathedral.

WORCESTER AREA

ales of ghosts, apparitions, demons and all things paranormal are as old as recorded history. One of the earliest in Worcester goes back over a thousand years, and concerns the church of Saint Mary, now completely disappeared but which once stood next to the cathedral to the north of the choir.

The story of Saint Mary's began when the Archbishop of Canterbury was frozen to death while crossing the Alps in 959 AD on his way to visit the Pope. His successor appointed Oswald, a handsome young man, of noble birth and high ideals, as Bishop of Worcester. Oswald's position was not an easy one. First, there were two rival religious communities in Worcester. There were those of Saint Peter's, built in 680, with its royal burial ground, who were at loggerheads with the clergy of Saint Mary's, nearby. Secondly, both parties appear to have had a preference for food, drink and women, and Oswald was a Benedictine. He believed in celibacy, obedience, labour and worship.

For many years, Oswald gently nudged the clergy into his way of thinking. Finally, in about 983, he decided to build a new church, Saint Mary's, next door to the old wooden cathedral of Saint Peter's. He transferred the bishop's chair from Saint Peter's to Saint Mary's so that Saint Mary's became the new cathedral.

Bequests and donations poured in, laying down the wealth of the church. It was the custom, among the wealthy, to give a donation to the church in the understanding that the donor was looked after in his old age.

Saint Oswald and the Devil

During the building he instructed his workers to use a large square stone lying nearby; but despite the efforts of eighty men, so the story goes, it could not be moved. Then Oswald prayed that the reason for its immovability should be known to him. Immediately, his eyes were opened and he saw, sitting upon the stone, a little black devil who was making obscene gestures at the workmen. Oswald exorcised the evil spirit by the sign of the cross and the stone was easily lifted by three men.

Oswald held the See of Worcester for 29 years (962-991) and for nineteen of these years (972-991) he was also Archbishop of York but he spent most of his time at Worcester and was brought there to die in 992. He was buried in Saint Mary's. After his death miracles began to be performed at his tomb and he was eventually canonised. One monk had a cancerous ulcer on one of his cheeks. On the Feast of Saint Oswald the monk drank out of a cup from which the saint used to drink, and when he had emptied it, he clapped it to his cheek and held it firmly there for a while. When he took it away all the cancerous growth stuck to the cup and his cheek was normal except for the fact that the one cheek was always a little ruddier than the other. When a great plague hit the city, the monks, praying and singing hymns, carried Oswald's corpse round the walls of the city. It was said that the plague immediately left Worcester and the surrounding villages.

Saint Mary's and Saint Peter's stood side by side for over sixty years, until they were burned down by the Danes in about 1041. Worcester was then without a cathedral for more than 40 years, until Saint Wulstan began to construct another in 1084. All that now remains of his building is the crypt.

Apparitions at Saint Helen's

At the time of the Doomsday survey in 1068 there were only three churches in Worcester, apart from the cathedral – Saint Helen's, Saint Martin's and Saint Andrew's. Saint Andrew's was rebuilt in 1751 but only the perpendicular tower has been left standing next to the riverside car park. The delicate spire is known locally as 'The Glover's needle', Worcester being famous for glove-making. The legend is told that when it was first built, it was on the other side of the river but the angels moved it to its present position during the night.

Perhaps Saint Helen's, near to Waterstones in the High Street, has the oldest church site, dating back to 680. It is believed by some historians to stand on the site of a Roman Temple. The early Christians, instead of opposing heathen traditions, whenever possible incorporated them into Christianity, consequently there is a possibility that they respected the site as holy ground but converted a Roman Temple into a Christian Church. It could have been named Helena after Flavia Julia Helena, wife of the Roman Emperor Constantius Chlorus and mother of Constantine the Great, who died in 328.

Saint Helen's, perhaps the oldest church in Worcester, is haunted.

Until the twentieth century, only the well-to-do had clocks and church bells were important. Saint Helen's bell tolled for fifteen minutes every morning at four o'clock to tell people that it was time to get out of bed, a custom which continued until about 1750. At eight o'clock in the evening the curfew bell rang, after which it gave the date by tolling one stroke for each day of the month. This was discontinued as recently as 1930.

The present church is mainly early Victorian and contains a monument to the famous Dud Dudley. From 1950 until 2001, it was used to house the Worcestershire archives. Now that it stands empty, we can reveal that it was haunted. The nave of the church has had a long tradition of being occupied by the ghost of a little girl who is looking for something. One lady saw her by a pillar downstairs not long after the 1950 renovations. The little girl spoke and said that she had lost her collection. A monk has been seen several times. A young man was working on a computer when he exclaimed, 'Something black has just brushed past me!'. One of the archival employees was in her late teens and had only been working at Saint Helen's for a short time when, on the Friday before Mothering Sunday, she bought a bunch of flowers during her lunch-time. At the end of the day she was the last to leave, she locked up then realised she had left the flowers inside. She unlocked, went back into the church and, to her horror, saw a dark figure of a monk near an interior door. She grabbed the flowers and flew out.

Perhaps the figure was that of Winsinus, returning to inspect the new developments. In Saint Oswald's days he was the vicar of Saint Helen's and he was also provost of the cathedral of Saint Peter's. In 959 Oswald finally persuaded him to become a monk and it was Winsinus who handed over the keys and all the possessions of Saint Peter's to Saint Oswald's new church of Saint Mary's.

Murder at Oddingley

The senior assistant at the county archives, Robin Whittaker, has never seen anything unusual at Saint Helen's but he did have a strange experience at Oddingley Church. Unfortunately, the church is remembered chiefly not for its stained glass, some of which goes back to 1500, or its seventeenth century tower, but for the fact that the Rector was murdered in 1806. He was too enthusiastic about collecting his tithes, and so five of the parishioners planned to murder him. They hired a wheelwright and carpenter, Thomas Heming, who shot his victim in broad daylight, was spotted in the act, and fled to the farm of one of the conspirators. There, they lost patience with him, killed him and buried him under the floor of the barn. In 1830, Heming's brother-in-law was hired to develop the barn and what should he find under the floor but the body of his long lost relative. The whole story came to light, but by then two of the conspirators had died. Only one was ever tried and he was acquitted. Robin Whittaker says:

> When I was a boy, one of our regular weekend activities was visiting local Worcestershire churches as all the family were interested in local and family history even then. It was one of the ways I have stored up knowledge of the county over the years. I think my father had heard of the Oddingley murder and had decided to visit the church.
>
> One sunny summer afternoon my family, comprising my father, mother, sister and I decided to go for a walk to Oddingley Church. As I went through the gate into the church yard I had a violent nosebleed and we had to stop for a few minutes while I received first aid.
>
> We went to the door of the church and we heard ethereal organ music, coming from the church. All of my family heard it. I'm afraid we didn't have the courage to go in. We turned back and went home.

My uncle decided he would prove us wrong concerning any paranormal activity and went back to the church. He was mortified when he discovered that there was no organ in the church, although later he did find a small harmonium but this could not have made the music we all heard.

Cromwell and the Devil

Although Saint Helen's suffered a major conversion, Worcester's splendid town hall has been preserved and is still in use. The Guildhall, in the High Street, was completed in 1723. Worcester was fiercely Royalist during the Civil War of 1642-1646 and the Battle of Worcester which took place on 3rd September, 1651. The head above the entrance doorway is said to be that of Cromwell, shown as a horned devil and nailed by his ears. There's an old legend that, on the morning of the battle, Cromwell sold his soul to the devil in Nunnery Wood for victory and seven years good fortune. He died on 3rd September 1658.

Cromwell's head, on the Guildhall.

Lost – One Ghost

When the house in the next story was demolished it left one ghost homeless. Sheila Armishaw says that she was about ten years of age when all this happened and she is now 80.

My grandmother was Jane Rogers and her house was at 34 Tybridge St. It was a very old house, some windows were bricked up on the landing and that goes back to the 1800s sometime. It's been knocked down and a petrol station stands on the site.

Although I never saw the ghost I have five sisters and they all saw her. How it came to light was that one day, my grandmother said to my grandfather, 'The girls are being silly, they say the house is haunted' to which my grandfather replied, 'That's right, I have seen her twice'. He was a retired policeman and very down-to-earth. When he saw her she was standing in front of the window. He fiddled with the curtains thinking it was a shadow or something. She used to come into a large back bedroom on the first floor. I slept in that room once and I didn't see her but I woke up crying bitterly. I had this tremendous feeling of sadness.

We didn't mind her at all, she was quite harmless. We called her Esther. She was middle-aged and wore old-fashioned clothes, a black blouse and a black skirt with a white collar. She came quite regularly and would walk to the side of the bed and look down at the occupant. She seemed to be looking for someone, we thought perhaps it could be a child.

A friend of my mother's stayed and she said, 'I know you came into my room in the night to see if we were alright but I didn't speak to you as my daughter was asleep'. No-one had gone into her room. The people who lived in the house before us had two sons and we were told that they both saw her.

A vicar came and prayed in the room and afterwards my grandmother put up the picture, 'Jesus of all Nations' but it didn't stop her coming.

My two aunts lived in the house after my grandmother died until the house was demolished in the 1970s. I often wonder where Esther is now and what happened to her when the house was turned into a petrol station.

The Evil Force

Some minor details have been changed in the following strange and sinister story to avoid identifying the road and the family in question.

A few years ago some friends of ours bought a house near the site of the 1651 battlefield, not far from the river Teme. My husband and I went to visit them, and as I walked into the house I thought, 'This is awful. There's something terrible about this place'. I tend to be sensitive to environments but this is the only time I have ever felt like that.

There was a large fire going and everybody else was roasting but I was freezing cold. I walked round the house, the entrance by the front door had been drastically renovated and I felt that was where the force was centred. It was terrible, absolutely terrible, I really felt as if it was evil and bad. You don't know what to do in a situation like that. Should I say something to the family and recommend that they had their house blessed? They must have thought it was perfectly alright or they wouldn't have bought it.

They had a beautiful dog and it was not long after our visit that their dog died mysteriously. The children were always ill. Then something awful happened, an acquaintance who was visiting the house had a heart attack and died in their garden, he wasn't all that old. Then the wife had a bad car accident. The husband fell off a ladder and was partly paralysed.

Eventually, I spoke to her about it. I said that I had felt that there was something the matter with the house and it should be blessed with a service by a minister. I was just patted on the head, so to speak, thanked for my advice and nobody took any notice of me.

The next time I went to back to the house I stood on the front doorstep and tried to talk to this force. This was something I had never done to that extent before. I didn't actually speak to it but it was as if there was a tickertape in my head, somebody was typing the words out and they kept coming. I felt that his name was Edmund.

At some stage one or two close friends of ours discovered how I felt and they told me that the house was built on the site where the old gallows used to be in Worcester. This was one explanation that made me feel quite creepy. Was some poor soul who had been left to rot on the gallows, wandering around, looking for a Christian burial?

I was glad that I had done my best to help. Later, the family moved out of the house.

Last year I was driving along their old road and I wasn't taking any notice of where I was, it hadn't crossed my mind that I was near to my friend's old house, when suddenly I saw a shape in the road. At first I thought it was a person on a bicycle going across the road and I was going to hit him. I slammed on my brakes but he just disappeared. Then I had that strange feeling again that he was Edmund. I thought, 'He's still round'. I just knew that he was one of these agitated souls who would benefit from some kind of a proper Christian burial.

Many Happy Returns

Julie* lives in a new house near the city centre.

In the spring of 1998 I was standing at my desk one day, tidying up, when I knew that somebody had come in through the front door. I thought it was my husband so I didn't bother to turn round. Then a chair was knocked over, I looked round and saw this stranger standing there. He was fairly tall, quite a big man, with dark hair, brown eyes and a big, bushy black moustache, the kind you see in that old poster

'Your Country Needs You'. He had a wing collar and was wearing a waistcoat. He was quite solid, I couldn't see through him, he looked as if he was made from gauze and the edges were quite misty. I was a bit taken aback. I thought, 'I don't know this person at all'.

I told my mother and she said, 'When was this?' I told her, 'Last Tuesday'. She said, 'That was your grandfather and it was his birthday'. My mother rummaged around and took out a photograph of her parents' wedding day. I knew straight away that my visitor was the groom. I hadn't seen the picture before, they didn't take many photographs in those days and this was the only one she had of him.

He died donkeys years ago, before I was born, and he lived in London. I have all his paintings here, perhaps he came to have a look at them. I was pleased to think he had come to visit me.

Worcester from the north-east. From an engraving by J Ross, 1816.

The Dog in the Night Time

From Worcester railway lines branch out in three directions. One line goes north to Droitwich then divides for Kidderminster or Birmingham, a south eastern line divides for Evesham or Cheltenham while a south-western line runs to the Malverns and Ross-on-Wye. Rebecca* moved into a house near one of these lines four years ago.

I was drawn to the house and it took me only 10 minutes to decide to buy it. At that time I had two large dogs. After about two weeks of moving in, one of them Suzie, started to lie at the bottom of the stairs looking up at the landing as if she had seen someone. She would sit up, wagging her tail, and then disappear upstairs into the front bedroom where she would lie on my bed. Night after night she would do this, as soon as I came home from work. It got to the point where I had to go upstairs and coax her back downstairs.

One Wednesday evening (Suzie was actually downstairs), I heard footsteps coming down the stairs. They were heavy and they stopped halfway down. At that point, I turned towards the door to see who it was but I saw nothing. Suzie went up the stairs for another evening on my bed. By this time, for some reason, I had named Suzie's invisible friend 'Bertie'. I only had to say to her, 'Where's Bertie?' and off she would go.

The very next evening I was vacuuming around my bed when I felt a sharp prod in my back. I turned round immediately but nothing was there. This happened again in the garden. I was not the only one who felt things. One evening a friend of mine was sitting on the settee with me when he felt 'something' pass through him. I was as warm as toast but my friend was freezing.

Suzie's personality changed drastically and I began to get worried about her. She became very destructive, such as getting bits of wallpaper in her teeth and tearing it off the wall. The first major episode concerned the water pipes in the bathroom. When I went to work I would leave the doors throughout the house open so that the dogs could move around. One day, I came home mid-afternoon but no Suzie greeted me at the back door – this had never happened before. I immediately panicked and went searching for her. I got to the lounge and saw water trickling through the ceiling, the carpets were soaking. I raced upstairs to find my bathroom carpet drenched and Suzie's teeth marks in the copper piping, the downpipe had been torn out.

I won't go into the repair bills plus two months of a dehumidifier plus redecorating. Now I was in major despair. I would sit on my bed and ask Bertie to pack it in. I began to close the bedroom door but Suzie must have scratched to get in because she ripped the carpet up. I thought of moving.

It came to a head one Saturday morning when I returned from the supermarket. No Suzie at the back door. I called her but nothing. I dropped my shopping and raced in, screaming and shouting for her. My other dog watched in awe. I found Suzie behind my futon in the back bedroom looking totally mesmerised. It took a couple of minutes before she came back to me. I managed to get her out from behind the futon, I don't know how she got into such a tiny space. Then I noticed the socket. She had managed to tear out a double socket from the wall behind the futon. To this day I will never understand why she wasn't electrocuted. That was it. I couldn't take it any more. I was a nervous wreck. I took Suzie down to the vets and she was put on tranquillisers.

Some friends of mine said that they knew some people who could help me. They came to the house one evening and walked round the house with me. I was standing in the back bedroom when one of them

An old view of Worcester, showing the west end of the cathedral, part of the city walls and the castle mount (now demolished).
From an engraving by P Sandig 1778.

11

asked if I knew an Albert. I froze. 'Bertie' is a nickname for Albert. They told me that Bertie had worked at a railway station nearby many years before and each evening he had left work to go down to the pub. My house had been built over an old pathway running from the station to the pub. However, the ground had been lowered to take the houses so that the pathway would have run through my front bedroom and out through the back. Where the footpath would have entered the bedroom was a large patch on the inside wall with cracked and discoloured plasterwork, and where it left the back bedroom was a similar patch on the wall. On his travels Bertie's spirit had marked the wall where he entered and where he made his exit. My guests that evening managed to prevent Bertie from walking through the house.

The footsteps stopped but Suzie was still very destructive. Another group of people arrived and they asked me if I knew a little girl, about nine years old. At this point it becomes a personal matter which I won't go into too deeply but, to cut a long story short, they told me that the little girl was following me around. Had I moved house, the little girl would have gone with me. My visitors assured me that she, too, had gone but two weeks later I could feel that she was back.

Every time I left for work I was worried sick, wondering what destruction I would find when I returned home. I asked the visitors to come back and, one evening, we all sat in my lounge. I was on the settee, a candle was burning on the table and I felt this little girl standing in front of me for a good 30 seconds. I felt her pass through me and as I watched the candle, the flame flickered frantically and then the little girl was gone. She has never returned and we are back to normal now. Part of me thought it was sad that Suzie had lost a friend, and she would stand at the bottom of the stairs as if waiting to be called.

These events went on for some eighteen months. Suzie is now on her own (my other dog passed away last year) and I have no problems with her. Why? How has it changed?

Through my visitors and various acquaintances I have discovered that I myself am partly responsible for Suzie's bad behaviour. I know that I am slightly psychic and I have been told that I am capable of 'mind travel'. There's one friend in particular and, by thinking about him, I can get him to telephone me within the next few seconds. I amuse colleagues at work by telling them, when their phone rings, who is on the line before they pick up the receiver. By worrying about Suzie's behaviour, I was causing her to be destructive. My mind caused her to do the things that she did. I made her do it. It wasn't Bertie and it wasn't the little girl – it was me. Now, whenever I leave this house, even for ten minutes, I close the lounge door and move my settee up to the door. That way I know that Suzie cannot push the door open, therefore I do not have to worry about any damage she could be doing elsewhere in the house.

Writing this fills me with dread that it will reopen my can of worms and I pray that this episode is closed.

One aspect of this worried me, if I am able to have this effect on animals, what effect could I have on people? I try desperately to think only nice things about people. If I was angry with someone, I hate to think what could happen.

Powick Bridge.

When the Battle's Lost (Powick)

Few villages have played such an important part in England's history as Powick. It was here, in the thirteenth century, that Simon de Montfort is thought to have taken Henry III prisoner. The first skirmish of the Civil War took place near Powick Bridge in 1642, when Prince Rupert's men routed a party of Cromwellians who surprised them resting in a field. The horrific Battle of Worcester in 1651 took place at several sites in and around the city and Powick Bridge was one of them. By the end of the battle three thousand lay dead throughout Worcester and the flat fields around the bridge were red with blood. Ten thousand were taken prisoner and two thousand were missing.

Powick village.

One of Powick's residents admits that there are many ghosts in the village:

> Even the butcher has a ghost. I was waiting in the queue at the butcher's one day and someone pushed me aside to make room for another person and when I turned round nobody was about. Several of the old houses have ghosts. I went to a meeting in one of these old houses when the speaker suddenly stopped and turned the colour of a refrigerator. Apparently, he had heard a voice behind him saying, 'Oh shut up, you do go on' but when he turned round no-one was there.
>
> Our house was built in 1694 and we have a ghost. Over the years my wife and I have sat in our drawing room and out of the corner of our eyes we have seen a dark shape going up the stairs. We have always assumed it was one of our cats rushing upstairs or something. On more than one occasion this has happened when the cats have been shut away and when there have been no children in the house. Neither of us said anything to the other, at risk of being thought stupid. Then one night we both saw it.
>
> The son of the previous occupier came past one day and he asked us if he could look round the house. His old bedroom is at the top of

the stairs which is now my son's room. He said, 'Have you heard the ghost? I used to lie in bed here and hear him going up and down the stairs'. This was in the days before the stairs were carpeted.

No doubt quite a lot went on here in times gone by. There certainly is a presence but it's a nice presence. This is a very happy house.

Guarding the Bridge for 350 Years

The Royalists held the bridge for two hours during the Battle of Worcester until they were cut off. Occasionally, an apparition from the Battle makes an appearance, as in the following anecdote by Margery:

In 1948 I had been on a cycling holiday round Devon and Cornwall, staying at Youth Hostels, with my husband, my friend and her husband. The two women were each on the back of a tandem, with the husband at the front.

We were coming home and going over Powick bridge when suddenly, about six yards away, we saw the top half of a Cromwellian-type soldier standing by the wall of the bridge. He looked quite solid, but you could only see his top half. He had lots of brown curls and a flat metal hat with a brim. He was only there for second or two, then he had gone. Our husbands didn't see it but my friend and I both saw it and we gasped, looked at each other and said, 'Did you see that?'

Wandering Ghosts (Callow End)

Powick merges into Callow End about four miles south of Worcester. Callow End is marked by the great red and white striped tower of Stanbrook Abbey. A Benedictine nunnery for English ladies had been founded at Cambrai in 1625, but they were expelled in 1808. The nuns moved to Salford Hall in Salford Priors (Worcestershire), earning a living by converting it into a girls' school, but in 1838 they settled at Stanbrook Abbey where they founded a Benedictine Nunnery. There was already an old building on the site and the new monastery was begun in 1878.

Occasionally, a ghostly nun seems to stray from the Abbey. Mr Long says that his grandparents lived at Callow End in the 1930s and did their courting near Stanbrook Abbey:

They were walking back along the Upton Road arm in arm when they saw what appeared to be a nun approaching them. The figure got closer and went between the two of them without unhooking their arms.

Local roads apparently play host to a variety of ghosts. In the early 1960s, Jean* and her husband saw an unusual figure:

One foggy and misty morning we came down the lane towards Stanbrook Abbey and there, right in the middle of the road was this shape. First of all I thought it was a cow in the road then I realised it was a man in a long belted mac. He just stood there, without moving, sideways on, right in the middle of the car's path so that you had to drive either side of him. As we went past it gave me such a funny sensation. I said to my husband, 'What do you think that was?' At that time there was a mental home not far away and we thought it might be someone from there but we asked around and nobody else had seen this man.

Ray Loveslife-Brown heard a strange story from a friend:

In the mid 1980s a friend of mine was seeing a girl in Callow End. If you know Callow End you will know that there is a very sharp bend and on the right is an old hall known as Wheatfield, now converted into flats. The girlfriend lived in a mobile home at the back of the old hall and my friend was walking towards the hall on the same side of the road. As he came to the corner he saw, walking in the opposite direction and on the other side of the road, an elderly woman in a tweed suit. She had on a jacket and woollen skirt (both tweed), brogues and a tweed Fedora hat. He heard a car coming up behind him, turned round briefly to take a quick look at the car, looked back again and in that second he heard the car slam its brakes on. He turned round to see what the matter was. The driver put his head out of the window and shouted, 'Where's that bloody stupid woman gone?' My friend asked, 'Which old woman?' and the driver replied, 'That old woman who walked right out in front of me'. He got out of the car and they both had a quick look round but there was nothing. On the right you are opposite the entrance to Wheatfield Hall and there are open fields on the left, it is quite clear all round except for the entrance and she could not have got across the road in that second.

Stanbrook Abbey, Callow End.

Prior Occupants

On the edge of Callow End, hidden behind huge ancient hedges, is Priors Court. The house once belonged to Lord Beauchamp, a descendant of the Earls of Warwick. The Prior is next in rank to an abbot, and where there is no abbot, the prior is head of an establishment, entrusted with the management of the property, the discipline of the monks and so on. Perhaps this house is where the old Priors of Callow End held court.

If all the legends and stories are to be believed, life at Priors Court has been as eventful as that of the villagers. A young member of the family is thought to have committed suicide when she was crossed in love, an old lady is said to have been battered to death while sheltering from the rain, one sister is believed to have killed another in a dispute over money and, when building alterations were taking place, one of the missing Royalists was found stuffed up a chimney.

In existence are copies of three documents, each signed and dated. The first is by the temporary caretaker, B E Huckfield, and is dated August 1905. He had only been resident for nine days when:

> At about 4.25 a.m., 28th August 1905, while sleeping in the bedroom above the dining hall at Priors Court, I was awakened by what appeared to me, in my semi-conscious state, by a noise as though a large heap of rough gravel had been suddenly upset outside the door which opens out on the back stairs, and is immediately opposite the door of the lumber room. The noise not being repeated however, and

seeing by my watch in the dim light of the morning what time it was, I persuaded myself that it was merely a trick of the imagination, or that some slight sound outside had been magnified by my half-aroused senses. By the time I had arrived at these conclusions I was thoroughly awake, I must have lain still for about five minutes, when suddenly the noise came again, louder than before, and apparently from the same spot. I at once sprang out of bed, and rushing across the room flung open the door. As I did so I saw a mist-like figure of about the proportions of a human body passing through the lumber room. Starting forward I followed it quickly through that room, and along the corridor to the bathroom. As I turned the corner there it vanished at the end of the corridor and door of the bedroom adjoining, but seeing nothing, considered that further search would be useless. One thing which struck me as being particularly curious was that the apparition appeared to cast a faint luminous shadow, if such a term may be allowed, on the right-hand wall of the corridor only. The light seemed very similar to the softened glow of an electric lamp. After satisfying myself that there was nothing more to be seen, I went back to bed, and though lay awake till it was time to rise, heard no repetition of the noise.

Almost a year later, Mrs Abbott, a young Scots lady, arrived on her honeymoon. Lady Beauchamp had visited her previously to warn her that the house was haunted 'but not being subject to nervousness I took no notice of what was said to me', a sentiment which she was soon to regret:

On Saturday, July 14th, between 1 and 2 a.m., I woke up in a cold perspiration, and I felt someone by my bed. I got a light and looked about, but could see nothing, and when daylight came thought it must have been my imagination, so decided to say nothing about it to anyone, but the following night I was talking to a maid in her room about 9.20 p.m. when we were called downstairs. I started alone, but when I reached the landing I distinctly saw the figure of a woman dressed in an Empire gown. I shrieked with fright, and fell rather than walked downstairs. On hearing my shrieks the maid quickly came downstairs and asked what was the matter. I told her I had seen the figure of a woman, but she laughed at my fears and did not believe me then, but at 10.30 p.m., the same night, four or us were sitting in the kitchen when suddenly I felt very cold, but was quite composed when the apparition appeared again, this time with uplifted arms, and pointed to the garden. I got up and said 'Well?'. It answered, 'Garden, money, woman, brick' and glided away. It terrified me so much I do not know what happened for the next hour, but when I came to myself the people that were in the room with me said they never saw or heard anything, but saw me get up and speak to it.

On July 24th at 8 p.m., I was in a room upstairs and happened to turn round, (the air seemed very cold) when I saw the same figure again. She stood for a minute, smiled at me then glided away.

Mrs Abbott was the seventh child of a seventh child which, according to tradition, gives her psychic powers.

Another statement is from Mrs Archdale who, in 1906, was looking for a country house to rent when she saw Priors Court advertised in 'Country Life'. When she visited the property she found a most attractive-looking house, but when she expressed interest she was visited by Lady Beauchamp who asked if she had been told about the ghost. She said that several people had seen the figure of a gentle-looking lady in grey, walking in different parts of the house. Village tradition said that it was one of two sisters who had quarrelled about some 'treasure' and that the one had murdered the other. Mrs Archdale nevertheless decided to rent the house. One night she heard the steady rustling of a silk dress going through the room. When she mentioned this to her husband, he said that he had also heard it previously.

Her eldest son, who was fourteen, was away at school during the term, but came home to Priors Court for the Christmas holidays. One night, she sent him to bed as usual at 9 p.m., then heard him screaming with fright. She rushed upstairs and found him half-dressed outside his bedroom door with his dogs. He told her that he had seen the ghost of a man in his bedroom.

Mrs Archdale was reluctant to terminate her tenancy and she decided instead to have the house exorcised. As her statement is the final one, this appears to have been successful.

An Easter Card Saves a Life (Bromyard)

Bromyard is about ten miles west of Worcester, just inside the Herefordshire border. In Saxon times, it was the third most important town in Herefordshire after Leominster and Hereford. The Bishops of Hereford built a palace here which has completely disappeared. The north and south doorways of the church are of Norman work in all its glory, and most of the building is medieval. The divorcee who tells the next story has chosen to buy a house in this lovely domain:

I was divorced some years ago and as my daughter is at college up north, I live on my own. One Good Friday, as usual, I sent her an Easter card. In the early hours of the morning her card fell off the shelf onto the carpet and in so doing made a noise which woke her up. Immediately she thought, 'Something is wrong with mother, I mustn't let anything happen to mother'. There was a clock on the shelf and she happened to notice the time.

At that precise moment I woke up to find the bedroom on fire. I know the exact time because I looked across the bed and noticed the clock on the bedroom wall. I managed to get to the telephone to dial 999 but the fire was so severe that it damaged my lungs. The firemen said that an oil heater in the bedroom had caught fire. Another three minutes and I would have died.

Bromyard, on the borders of Herefordshire.

BEWDLEY AREA

n 1425 the riverside town of Bewdley became the property of Richard, Duke of York. Later that century the Wars of the Roses developed, with the Lancastrians taking the red rose and the Yorkists the white for their badges. Richard's fortunes waxed and waned, but the town remained loyal to him and when his son proclaimed himself King in 1461, Bewdley received many rewards. It was, for example, granted the privilege of a sanctuary town, and anyone within its boundaries was beyond the arm of the law. This proved to be a mixed blessing, as the town found itself hosting many villains. Respectable people resided by the river while those escaping justice lived further up the hill, too far for the local henchmen to drag them across the bridge. A small district on the Kidderminster side of the bridge is named Catchem's End and below the bridge is Whispering Street, where fugitives waited until darkness so that they could cross the river and reach sanctuary.

The Legend of Blackstone Rock

On the river Severn about a mile south-east of Bewdley is the prominent Blackstone Rock, riddled with caves once used by hermits and smugglers. A romantic story has grown around them of which the following is one of the many versions:

A beautiful young lady by the name of Alice was to be married to Sir Harry Wade. As she was on her way to the wedding, a young man on a horse snatched her and carried her off. The wedding party was in hot pursuit and when they started gaining at Deritend the young

Until the late eighteenth century Bewdley was a great trading centre.

man threw the bride into the river Rae where she was drowned. The young man managed to reach Bewdley, where he obtained sanctuary. Sir Harry Wade never recovered from his loss and became a hermit at Blackstone Rock. The years passed, then one day, a man went to see him to confess his sins. He said that, many years before, he had admired a lady but had been too shy to declare his love. He had snatched her on her wedding day and galloped away with her. Her name was Alice. With that, Sir Harry leaped at him and pushed him over the edge of the cliff to his death.

In Holy Trinity Church, Stratford-upon-Avon, are the tombs of the Clopton family. They were at their height in 1491, when Hugh Clopton was Lord Mayor of London. One of the tombs is without an inscription and it is thought that the occupant may be the young man who abducted the bride.

Blackstone rock, haunt of many romantic legends.

Spirited Elections

There was never any love lost between the inhabitants of Bewdley and Stourport-on-Severn. Before 1772, Bewdley was the great trading centre of the Midlands, with goods travelling along the river Severn to be taken to and from the Midlands and the Black Country. Stables accommodated as many as four hundred pack horses and one in six of the houses was a hotel for travellers. When Brindley's canal arrived the trade was taken away from Bewdley. Stables and inns stood empty. Bewdley watermen sent a petition to the Stourport landowner asking him not to sell the land to build a bridge over the river, as they were already paying more than half their wages – 10/6d (52p) in the £ – to support the poor and a bridge at Stourport would impoverish them even further.

Bewdley was the home of the Tories while Stourport-on-Severn was passionately Whig. When the results of the elections were to be announced, the young men of Stourport would tramp to Bewdley armed with sticks, and fighting was so severe the night would end with many cracked skulls.

In the general election of June 2001 all parties were concerned about voter apathy and low turnouts. A hundred and fifty years ago problems arose not from apathy, but from over-enthusiasm. The fact that local people were able to have an input into the running of the country was a new and exciting idea which only came into existence in 1832. In 1867 even people on a low income were allowed to vote. Elections were corrupt, violent and bloody affairs. Voting in secret had not yet arrived and so a man's political views were well-known. Voters were bribed with money, free drink and other delights. One aim was to get members of the opposing side so drunk they were unable to vote.

In January 1969, Sir Richard Attwood Glass, the Conservative candidate for Bewdley and Stourport-on-Severn, was to attend court, charged with corruption at the preceding elections.

The Kidderminster Times of January 23rd 1869 states that 'at an early hour the streets presented an animated appearance, and the witnesses, and others interested in the case, flocked in from Stourport and the outlying places…'

> A large crowd had assembled at the entrance to the hall, and it was not easy for persons to pass in. This, unfortunately, led to a very melancholy incident, for during the crushing and excitement a police-constable, named Dovey, fell down a corpse. It appears he had been suffering from a diseased heart and this, with the excitement of the moment superadded, must have occasioned his death.

In the autumn of the mid-1990s, a lady who lives on the Tenbury Road in Far Forest was returning from a meeting when:

> About ten past ten I walked across the road just outside my house and I bumped into somebody. I went to say, 'Sorry' and then I suddenly realised that nobody was there. I definitely felt that I had bumped into

someone, it felt just as you do when you bump into a person in a crowd. A year or two later I happened to read a little booklet on the history of Far Forest in which it said that the first policeman was Mr Dovey, he died a violent death and it named his house, Friars Girth – which was ours!

PC James Dovey was 45 years old when he died and he had been in the police force for nearly 24 years.

A Ghost that Washes Dishes (The Running Horse)

The golden age of coaching lasted from 1820 to 1837. A coaching inn would have plenty of stables, repair sheds, ample public rooms and large numbers of bedrooms. On short distances, coaches were pulled by two horses but if the journey was of any length, four horses were used. By law, horses had to be changed at regular intervals and at important inns, and where men knew their jobs well, a team of coach horses could be changed in two minutes, sometimes fifty seconds.

The Running Horse is at least 300 years old, and was an old coaching inn on one of the main routes in and out of Wales. The end of the building nearest the bar is the old part and the kitchen is where the stable used to be.

The locals say that all the licensees have declared that the place is haunted. Richard and Chrissie arrived in October 2000. At first, their daughter was most unhappy:

I slept in an upper bedroom which had once been an office. I hated that room. It was always cold, even though the bed was next to the radiator. A few days after we moved in the TV in my bedroom switched itself off and refused to work. Four or five days later I bought a radio and that switched itself off. A few days after that I bought another radio and that switched itself off. The night before the TV switched itself off, I was watching Brookside and my mother was watching the same programme in the next bedroom so that I could hear it. There was a five second delay between the words from my mother's television and the words from my television. I would hear a phrase coming from my mother's room and the same phrase would be repeated in my room. After Christmas the room seemed to warm up and I'm now quite happy there.

Chrissie has another strange story:

> My daughter's partner works behind the bar and he lives with us. He woke up one day and had a massive toothache. I asked him if he wanted me to get him some Paracetamol and he said he would get some himself. Later that morning I went with my daughter to the village Co-op. I got to where the toiletries were and thought, 'I wonder if Darren has been able to get any Paracetamol?'. I decided that he must surely have bought some and so, without a doubt, I did not put any tablets in my shopping basket. However, when I put my basket on the cash-out, I lifted my odds and ends out of the basket and there was a box of Paracetamol. I said to my daughter, 'Have you put these in here?' and she said that she hadn't. I said, 'Well, how did they get in there then?'
>
> When Darren came home I asked him if he's been able to get some Paracetamol and he said that he'd been too busy, so I was able to give him a packet.

Ian works at the Running Horse as a kitchen porter whenever he comes back from his travels:

> I started working here in 1995, the management had just spent half a million pounds on extensive renovations and that's when most things happened.
>
> On one occasion I took a dirty plate out of the dishwasher, I turned round to put the cloth down and when I turned back the plate was just hanging there, in the air, and it was clean! The ghost had washed it! I ran out of the kitchen and said I wasn't going back. I have been working there when we should have heard piped music on the PA system but instead there was a little girl's voice. She started singing, then

The Running Horse has a playful ghost.

we could hear a man's voice in the background and the little girl would scream.

My sister started working there before me. Some of the things that happened to me also happened to her. One day, she was setting up the menus and laying the cutlery with Lisa, and she was talking to this figure, not concentrating properly on the conversation because she was working, when suddenly, the figure disappeared and she discovered that Lisa was in the kitchen. At that moment a strong wind went through the whole place, so strong that it blew the menus down, despite the windows and doors being closed.

On another day my sister said, 'I wish it would p... off' and a glass flew off the shelf, hit her in the arm and smashed on the floor.

The locals say that an elderly gentleman passed away in the alcove and his spirit has sometimes been seen there. My sister and I

Stourport-on-Severn, before the canal arrived it was a sandy waste.

have seen things but nothing definite. There was nothing that you could make out, not a discernible figure. You think, has something moved there or was it a shadow?

Other people working here have had problems. Four or five years ago Anne was working here and something was always happening to her. Her possessions were moved and sometimes they would be hidden. She said it was a playful ghost which was trying to wind her up.

The previous licensees, Dave and Margaret, had some guests over. When the pub was renovated, a lot of old books were put on the shelves. One of these guests said, 'This old book looks interesting', he pulled it down and it fell open at a page which had been signed by his grandmother. He had never seen the book before. Also, they had an old leather sandal that they kept throwing away but it kept reap-

pearing, on the back seat of the car, in the bedroom, in the house, everywhere. Margaret said that she sometimes went a long way from the house to throw it out but there it would be again.

I have taken three or four years off, travelling round the world, and when I came back everything was much better but it's still there. In the main bar is a big open fire, you're alright there but when you leave it to go to the bar you feel uncomfortable.

Chrissie adds: 'I've never felt that there's anything unpleasant here. I have been in here on my own a few times and I have never been afraid'.

Shades of Evening

The county boundary between Shropshire and Worcestershire runs between Far Forest and Cleobury Mortimer, with Far Forest on the Worcestershire side and Cleobury Mortimer just inside Shropshire. Margaret once lived near the border and not far from the Horse and Jockey:

Our house was called Little Oak and had been a woodcutter's cottage. It is still there. Two ladies used to live there who had the surname DeVit. With a name like that they must have been French and descended from the Huguenots. They lived there many years before I did. One evening, I saw one of them.

I was on my own with the baby when I noticed that our front gate was open. We had to keep the gate shut otherwise the pigs and cows used to come in so I went to close the gate. It was getting dusk, in our garden was a sycamore tree with an owl in it and the hooting of the owl made it really atmospheric. I was standing by the gate with the baby in my arms when I saw someone gliding diagonally across the front garden. She had a long skirt and a shawl over her head and she was wearing very dark clothes. I assumed it was one of the DeVits.

I have been on national service in Germany so it takes a lot to make me scared. I had always had the feeling that somebody else was in the garden.

STOURPORT-ON-SEVERN

Only three hundred years ago the site of Stourport-on-Severn was nothing but scrubland and sandy waste. Then James Brindley, one of England's first great civil engineers arrived on the scene. He decreed that the Staffordshire and Worcestershire canal should follow the valley of the river Stour and join the river Severn here. He planned a network of basins and locks but never saw his vision completed for he died of overwork and diabetes in 1771. Until about 1960 Stourport was a great industrial town, with large industries attracted by the abundance of water and ease of transport but these have now either closed or moved away from the centre of the town. From its inception Stourport has been popular as a holiday resort, now with many summer visitors, and eleven large caravan parks holding about 1,250 caravans.

Stourport Past and Presence

The Swan Hotel in Stourport-on-Severn played a leading role in elections, favouring the Whigs, or Liberals. Over the entrance was a balcony from which the speakers could expound their views to the excited and rowdy electors in the street below. Most people in Stourport voted Whig and the open space in front of the inn would be full of Whig supporters.

Vic Mitchley was licensee from 1958 to 1972:

> We had a ghost at the Swan. Late one evening I went into the office, which in those days was on the first floor, and I had the impression of someone behind the glass panel on the reception desk, waiting for attention. Our largest dog was with me and his hackles rose. I switched the light on, but nobody was there. I happened to mention this to my wife afterwards and she said, 'Oh, you mean the old lady who stands by the window, I've spoken to her several times'. She described her as wearing a bonnet, rather like those worn by the ladies of the Salvation Army.

Until 2001, Samantha's Flower Shop had been in the same family for years. Previously it was a barbers belonging to Bill Bickerton and his father before him. Bill says:

Something curious used to happen every night. We had four chairs in a row in the salon, and every night my father would insist that we shook the gowns out and lay them carefully across the chairs, stretching them across the arm so that the air could get in underneath to keep them sweet. Every morning when we arrived the third chair from the end would look as if someone had sat in it. The gown was pressed neatly against the sides. This used to tickle us pink. My father always joked about it.

Samantha's Flower Shop is now the Flower Cellar.

Older residents will remember Mr Trapp who ran the post office at Areley Kings until 1953. He always declared that, a few years before he retired, he was walking to Worcester and was at Ridley's Cross when a grey lady drifted across the road in front of him and went into a copse on the right hand side of the road. As he approached the spot where she had disappeared, he realised that there was no gate that she could have gone through. It was a quiet country road, darkness was falling and he found it quite a frightening experience.

Walking Through the Walls (Shrawley)

About four miles south of Stourport-on-Severn is Shrawley, a small village with a great history. In the late nineteenth and the twentieth century locks and reservoirs were built along the River Severn, raising the level and reducing the tidal flow. Previously, Shrawley was one of the few places where it was possible to ford the river. A castle here disappeared centuries ago, perhaps the ancient Britons fought the Romans on its slopes. Shrawley's rare lime-tree woods once sheltered many fugitives from the Civil War of 1841-6. Carved into the red rocks of the riverbank are a number of caves, once occupied by hermits who spent their leisure time rescuing unwanted babies from the river Severn, set adrift from Bewdley bridge.

Because of its history, Shrawley should be teeming with ghosts. A young couple were driving towards the village from Stourport when they saw a grey horse galloping along the road towards them. They thought they were going to hit the horse but to their amazement, it sailed into the air over the top of them. In an old, semi-detached cottage the residents are having problems:

> Nobody has seen anything here but there are a lot of strange noises and smells. I have definitely smelt lavender, quite strong, when there was no reason for it, then there's a smoky smell. One evening I felt something really strange. I felt that a middle-aged man was present who didn't like the change of occupiers in the house. It was really weird, I'm not into that sort of thing. I don't know whether it was the air pressure or something.

> At that time I was sleeping upstairs and a friend of mine was sleeping downstairs. I went upstairs to brush my teeth and when I went into the bathroom I smelt a funny, musty smell and I had the feeling that the presence was there. Suddenly, the light went out and after a couple of seconds, the light bulb exploded. I was out of there like greased lightning and that night I slept on the settee and my friend had to sleep on the floor.

> The people next door told us that their house is haunted with a grey ghost that walks between the houses. They said that it walks quite happily through the walls. They have now moved away so that the house is empty but we have heard strange noises coming from there, all kinds of squeaking and creaking.

> Just lately, it seems to be getting worse.

The Pattering of Tiny Feet (Hartlebury)

Hartlebury Castle has been the seat of the Bishops of Worcester since 1268 and their principal residence for four centuries. Many of the bishops who lived here have been at the heart of great British events, some even helped to change them. Bishop Latimer helped Henry VIII to obtain his divorce from Catherine of Aragon; Bishop Stillingfleet was Chaplain to Charles II.

At a meeting of Far Forest WI in the autumn of 2000, one of the members told this curious story:

A friend of mine, who is a very sane, sensible person, moved into an old cottage near Hartlebury Castle. She lived there for some months before she got around to cleaning out an old cupboard on the first floor corridor, outside her bedroom. There, at the back of the cupboard were a pair of child's flat silk shoes with a little bow on the front, obviously very old and possibly Victorian. They were in quite good condition and so she took them along to Hartlebury Museum.

That night, when she and her husband were going to bed, they heard the sound of what appeared to be footsteps pattering up and down the corridor several times. They thought nothing of it, perhaps it was a knocking of the pipes or a reverberation from somewhere. However, the next morning the cupboard door was open when she was sure she had closed it the previous evening. The next night, the same thing happened. Night after night they heard a child's footsteps going up and down the corridor outside.

She decided that the owner of the shoes was looking for them. She went to the curator at Hartlebury and said, 'I'd like to have the shoes back, please'. As soon as they were replaced in the cupboard the footsteps stopped.

A fascinating tale comes from Hartlebury.

BROMSGROVE AREA

he spire of Bromsgrove parish church dominates the view for miles around. In the early part of the tenth century the Midlands were ravaged by a Danish army. King Alfred's daughter, Athelflaeda, built a burgh at Bromsgrove, one of a chain of fortifications against the Danes. This was probably the hill on which the ancient church of Saint John the Baptist now stands. The original little Norman church has now almost entirely disappeared but in its place has risen a grand edifice in perpendicular splendour.

In the churchyard is the famous headstone to Thomas Scaife and Joseph Rutherford who died in 1840 when the boiler of a Birmingham and Gloucester Railway engine blew up. The first few lines of the poem on their tombstone reads:

> My engine now is cold and still
> No water does my boiler fill;
> My coke affords its flame no more,
> My days of usefulness are o'er.

Bromsgrove High Street, built along the line of an ancient trackway.

On top of the boundary wall on the north side of the churchyard was an old stone figure in a tunic with the hands in prayer. Tradition said that it was an individual who sold himself to the devil for certain advantages, consequently, when he died his body could not be buried either in or out of the churchyard. Before he died he made it known that he had to be buried under the churchyard wall and the figure placed on top. At one time, the saying, 'neither in or out' was quite common, for example, husbands were often told that they were not to drink either in or out of a house, which meant that they were not to drink at all. Each year, the figure moved slightly until it was twenty yards from its original position, said to be the devil's work. The figure has now disappeared. Most likely, the figure was on top of the wall because it was the custom sometime in the sixteenth or seventeenth centuries to give each local landowner a piece of the churchyard wall to keep in good repair, and occasionally the landowner used part of the wall as his memorial. Another example is at Areley King's Church, where Sir Harry Coningsby created his memorial.

Mrs Mop's Secret Admirer

Bromsgrove High Street is built along an ancient track which ran from Selly Oak in Birmingham to the Worcestershire Beacon on the Malvern Hills. Many of the buildings go back to the seventeenth century, a few could be even older. With such an ancient town, it is not surprising that staff in several of the shops complain of mysterious footsteps and invisible customers opening their shop doors. The owner of the shop in the following story has now retired:

> We had a shop in the Bromsgrove High Street on the site of a very old building, and we had some strange phenomena. This particular ghost used to take a liking to the cleaner's things, dusters and bowls. The dusters were kept in the staff room at the back but the cleaner would come in early in the morning and find them pushed down the back of the sink. We used to hear footsteps walk through the shop and go out the back way. The girls complained about inexplicable noises out the back and they refused to stay in the building on their own.
>
> We once lost a valuable ring. We turned the office inside out but we couldn't find it. Some months afterwards we happened to lose something which rolled under the cabinet. We pulled the cabinet out

and there was the ring. Yet we had looked under there and pulled the cabinet out several times.

A lady came into the shop one day and said, 'Do you know you have a ghost here?' I said, 'Possibly, what makes you think that?' She said, 'While I was standing here, I saw the ghost of a little old man'.

We only had a small staff and we had had them for a long time. I was the only one with the keys.

Aston Fields Industrial Estate.

In Another World (Aston Fields)

The Sugar Brook borders two sides of the Aston Fields Trading Estate. Across England are several brooks of this name, thought by historians to refer to a ceremony dating back to manorial times where sugar was sprinkled in the water on Palm Sunday, but the locals say that this brook arises from a spring which has sweet-tasting water. As it flows past the sewage works, tasting is not recommended.

Mike lives in Redditch but seven or eight years ago he was working in Bromsgrove in one of the Factory Units on the Trading Estate, near to Garringtons.

I was manager of the unit so I was working there on my own one night – it's 2,000 feet, not all that large. While I was working this guy just appeared. He had blue overalls, he was bald, and where he had a bit of hair left it was white. He was very modern-looking. I thought, 'I'm seeing things'. I shouted something like, 'Oi, come here!' to get his attention. He didn't look at me, he looked as if he was in another world. He took a dozen steps and then he disappeared. I saw him again, later, in all I saw him seven or eight times after that. It really shook me up.

A Short-Stay Patient (Blackwell Recovery Hospital)

Blackwell Recovery Hospital was probably built for soldiers during the first world war. Situated near the railway line, it has now completely disappeared and has been replaced by a housing estate. Rosemary was an auxiliary nurse there in the 1970s:

Blackwell Recovery Hospital was a lovely old place with a happy atmosphere. I enjoyed my time there so much that I went on to do the full nursing training and worked as a nurse for over twenty years.

The nursing staff used to take it in turns to go round every two hours to check the patients, administer the drugs and so on. I was on the 12 o'clock midnight round with Sister and it was my turn to do the locking up and checking the bolts and locks. When the following incident occurred we had just finished the round and I was taking the keys back to the key cupboard.

To get to the key cupboard I had to go through the reception hall where chairs were scattered about. Then I noticed, out of the corner of my eye, that there was an elderly lady sitting in one of the chairs. I was a bit surprised because we had just done the rounds and all the patients had been in bed. She wasn't even in her nightclothes. I only saw her for a brief moment but I had the impression that she was quite small and she had steel-grey curly hair which looked short from the front but I think it had been pulled back into a bun. She had a black shawl round her shoulders and her dress looked Victorian, it was dark with large sleeves. I couldn't see how long it was because she was sitting down.

I said, 'Oh my dear, you should have been in bed a long time ago – wait there and I'll be back in a minute to put you to bed'. I put the keys away in the cupboard which was only a few steps and when I turned round she had gone. I couldn't understand how she had managed to disappear so quickly. I said to the others who were in the next room, 'Where's that old lady gone?' and they said, 'Which old lady?'.

A Chartist cottage at Dodford.

Did You See Something Back There? (Dodford)

Dodford is only a tiny village, west of the junction of the M5 and M42, and is unusual in that although it is a historic village, most of the history only goes back two centuries. It was a Chartist village, the result of a fervent political movement in the mid 1800s. A document with a million signatures was presented to parliament, demanding six articles of legislation to improve the life of the ordinary working man, such as voting by ballot. Under one Chartist scheme, workers paid into a fund, land was bought with the proceeds and houses built with three acres of ground, supposedly to make the owner self sufficient so that he could escape the drudgery of low-paid, hard work. Names were drawn out of a hat to decide which workers should take possession of the houses. The movement ended in scandal in about 1854 when the organisers mismanaged the funds and thousands of workers lost their hard-earned investments.

The village also has one of the best Arts and Crafts churches in England. Designed by Arthur Bartlett and built in about 1907, Holy Trinity and Saint Mary contains carvings, lights, stained glass windows and statues by the Bromsgrove Guild. The Guild was founded in 1898 to produce high quality crafts and soon became world-famous. Two well-known pieces are the gates of Buckingham Palace and the Liver Birds in Liverpool.

Peter lives near Dodford and is a chef. In May 2000:

> I had finished work, had a couple of beers with the boss and rung for a taxi so it must have been about 12.30 at night when we were going along Warbridge Lane, this is only a little country lane at Dodford and we had nearly reached the T junction. It had been raining all day and was quite a murky evening. There was one car in front of us. Suddenly this black silhouette ran across the road from right to left. I'm six feet one inch and it was as tall as I am. The strange thing was that it wasn't gliding or floating or anything, you could see its legs going. The headlights of the car in front were straight on it, it wasn't shining or anything, just a solid matt black. The car obviously didn't see it and the black silhouette ran straight through the car. Then it stopped at the side of the road and suddenly it had gone.
>
> The taxi driver looked at me and said, 'Did you see something back there?' I said that I had. He asked 'What did you actually see?' I told him that I had seen something black run across the road. He said, 'I saw that but I didn't want to say anything in case you thought I was a bit peculiar or something'. So I wasn't the only one who saw it.

Housman and the Clock House (Cockburn)

About half a mile east of Dodford is Fockbury and the Clock House. It was here that Bromsgrove's pride and joy, the poet Alfred Edward Housman, spent his teenage years. Housman's grandfather was the local vicar and lived in the Clock House. Soon after the poet was born in 1859, the family moved to Perry Hall in the centre of Bromsgrove, where Housman's father practiced as a solicitor. After twelve happy years Housman's mother died. His father seems to have run into financial difficulties, consequently in 1872, when Housman was thirteen, the family went to live at the Clock House. The house has now been rebuilt but the old clock tower remains as Mr Sleigh, the present owner, explains:

> We moved here in the March of 1979 and we have been able to build a new, smaller house in the exact position of the Clock House. The house was very old, it was originally only a small cottage then it grew and grew. The old tower with its clock is still there in the garden, just a home for pigeons now. It was once part of the house.

The first night I was here I went into the tower and I felt as if some-one was there. The hair came up on the back of my neck. I thought, 'This is my imagination'. I have never felt anything like that before. The second night the same thing happened. This time I swore at it, I said, 'If you don't pack this up I will knock the tower down'. I never had any trouble after that except that I had two Alsatian dogs who followed me everywhere but they wouldn't go into the tower.

One day, a young man who used to live in the house came to visit with his fiancée. I said to him, out of curiosity, 'Did you ever feel anything strange in the tower?'. He told me that the tower scared him so much that he would never walk along the passageway that led to the tower on his own.

I have friends at Hill Farm in Rocky Lane and one of their in-laws is supposedly psychic. He came with his wife one day to look at the garden (we have seven acres). I took him into the tower and he said that there was a spirit present and he described it. He said that it was the gardener who used to wind the clock. We know that a series of gardeners have been employed here since 1610.

In the garden is a monument in memory of Mary Ann Scott who died here. I call her Aunty Annie. The psychic couple came along and the man started to shake like a leaf. I thought he was having a heart attack. He said, 'She's here, she's here!' I thought he meant Mary Ann Scott but he said, 'No, the nurse who nursed her' and he described her as wearing a crinoline and a bonnet. I couldn't see anything.

This couple went into the house and when they reached the dining room they said, 'This room is full of spirits'. I told them that if we put a plant or a bunch of flowers in there, two days later it was dead. They said that that was because the spirits were draining the life and energy of the plant. I said to the psychic couple that we have never felt uncomfortable in the house and they said that we wouldn't, these were loving ghosts, nothing bad has ever happened here.

My youngest daughter's bedroom is directly above the dining room. After the couple had left I asked her, 'When mum and I used to go out did you feel uneasy or uncomfortable in the house?'. She replied, 'Oh no, there was always someone in the house with me'. She had never said anything before.

The locals tell me that the house has the reputation of being haunted by a white lady. Evidently Jean Davidson, the JP for Bromsgrove used to live in the house and she often saw it. She called it, 'The Nanny' it used to walk through the wall regularly.

However, my wife and I have lived here for over twenty years and we have yet to see it.

My Grandfather's Clock (Catshill)

Although June lives in Redditch we have included her story here because of its relevance:

When my grandparents were married in about 1900 they bought this huge Ormolu clock in a domed glass case. It was their pride and joy and stood in the front parlour on a marble top with a mirror behind so that the workings of the clock were reflected in the mirror. When I was a little girl, as a special treat, I was occasionally taken in to see their marvellous clock ticking away. I was fascinated and they always promised that they would leave it to me in their will, although I remember wondering as a teenager what on earth I would do with it because at that time we were all into the modern Danish-style furniture. However, eventually my grandmother died, then my grandfather; the clock became mine and it suited my present home very well, in fact I had a special recess made for it.

Rod Healey has an unusual story about a grandfather clock.

The clock was wound up every Sunday and as it was an eight-day clock it never stopped – until one morning on the third of February. I sat down to have my breakfast and noticed that the clock had stopped at 3.45 in the morning. I couldn't think why this had happened and pondered for some days, until I suddenly remembered that this was my grandfather's birthday!

I had no more trouble with the clock for twelve months, but at exactly the same time this year, it stopped again. I'm waiting to see what happens next year.

Rod Healey is a clockmaker by trade, his shop is the Old Clock Shop at Catshill.

I hear these kinds of stories all the time, but what happened to me was quite different.

We had a telephone call from this old chap, could we go and collect a grandfather clock from his house and repair it? A small man with white hair answered the door and showed us the grandfather clock which had been badly damaged. Evidently, he and his wife were decorating and they had moved the clock so that it was propped up against the front door. The local paper had been shoved through the door and it pushed the grandfather clock over so that it had fallen and smashed against the banister rail.

He said that he was sorry that he hadn't been able to bring the clock to us but his wife was seriously ill upstairs and not expected to live. We discussed the price with him and everything was accepted. The clock needed a lot of work and was in the shop for about eight weeks. We restored the case and did the movements but the clock wouldn't go. Every now and then we had another attempt while we carried on doing various bits and pieces to it, but the clock wouldn't run.

At that time (around about 1986), I was living at the shop. We were very busy and I was working all hours. The kitchen had been converted into a workshop and I was there at about two or two-thirty in the morning when I had this funny feeling that I had to turn round and that somebody was there. Behind me was the dining area where the clock stood. I turned round and saw, through the open door, somebody standing by the clock. He was about five feet two inches in height and had white hair. He wasn't looking at me but he was facing the clock. I shot to the far end of the kitchen and grabbed a milk bottle, thinking that somebody had broken in. My heart was going bangettybang. When I looked back, nobody was there. I fled up the stairs to my flat. In the morning I wondered if it had actually happened or if I had imagined it. I opened the clock case and swung the pendulum and, do you know, it never stopped. For several weeks after that I was afraid to go into my shop at night.

When we took the clock back an old lady answered the door. She said that she was very sorry, she didn't know what arrangements had been made about paying the bill as her husband had since died. We told her that when we called previously, he had said that his wife was very ill and not expected to live. She said, 'Yes, that was me. I lived and my husband died'.

I wouldn't like to say with one hundred per cent certainty that the old man I saw by the clock was her husband as I only took a brief look at him, but he was certainly very similar.

Enchanted Tardebigge

Tardebigge church stands on a hill and it is 135 feet (about 41 metres) tall spire is a well-known landmark. The church was built in 1777 by Francis Hiorn after the previous spire had fallen down, and the chancel was modernised a hundred years later. From the church the ground

Saint Bartholomew's at Tardebigge.

drops steeply to the canal with the country's longest flights of narrow locks. Below the church was once a spring where the waters were thought to cure certain diseases.

A cutting from the Glastonbury thorn once flourished in the churchyard. Joseph of Arimathea is said to have come to Glastonbury in Somerset where, allegedly, his staff took root and grew into the Glastonbury thorn. The original tree, which only bloomed once a year on Christmas Day (some legends say Twelfth night), was destroyed by an enthusiastic Puritan, but cuttings had been distributed across England and one had arrived at Tardebigge. Oddly, the thorn is a Middle Eastern plant, not a British or European one. It would normally flower in mid-winter and, in olden days when people gathered around it with lanterns on Christmas Eve the warmth of the lamps was probably sufficient to guarantee its flowering.

A Military Presence

The cream of society lies in the churchyard. The tombs of the Earls of Plymouth are collected together by the front doors, the great British ambassador Sir Augustus Berkeley Paget (1823-1896) is nearby and a yard or two beyond the Plymouth memorials is a stately cross on a large plinth to Captain William Emmott. He died on the 14th April 1865 aged 74 years.

Captain Emmott's monument was erected by Baroness Windsor 'in grateful token of the zeal and energy evinced by him in the discharge of his duty as adjutant of the queen's own Worcestershire Yeomanry cavalry under her brother the Earl of Plymouth and her husband, the Hon R H Clive'.

Captain Emmott was the oldest serving adjutant ever in the British Army. His period of service would have covered the Battle of Waterloo (1815), the Crimean war, which began in 1854, the Indian mutiny of 1857 leading to the collapse of the East India company, and the first rumblings of unrest with South Africa which led to the Boer war.

The rambling old house once occupied by Captain Emmott is only a short walk from his tomb. The young couple who bought it in the early 1990s 'fell in love with it at first sight', despite its dilapidated state. The husband, Tom*, seems to have a strange affinity for the spirit of Captain Emmott for he has a military background. He had no idea that he had purchased the house of an army gentleman until he began to research into its history. However, it was his wife, Sarah*, who first sensed the strange presence.

> When we were first looking round the house I thought I felt a little something but I didn't mention it because we liked the house so much. We moved in about the beginning of June and the day after we moved in Tom had to go away with his work and I was left on my own for several weeks. It being a new place, I borrowed a friend's dog to keep me company. I was washing up when I clearly heard somebody going up the stairs. The footsteps went all the way up the three flights of stairs fairly quickly and quite purposefully. At first I thought it might be the dog but he was under the table. I took the dog with me while I had a look round and checked that there was nobody else in the house.

Captain Emmott's memorial.

Tom says that he had only been away two days when he had a call from Sarah:

> She said first that the range had gone out and she couldn't relight it, and secondly, what would my comment be about another person living in the house?
> I heard the footsteps when I came home. They would happen all times of the day, we often heard them. They were quite heavy and you could tell it wasn't a creaking stair.
> Occasionally, when a guest comes out of one of the middle front bedrooms, somebody or something – just a dark shape – goes in. Several guests have seen it, including my mother. She's convinced that it's a man but we tell her that it's wishful thinking at her age!

If you go into the toilet you are aware that someone has come up behind you. It's not malevolent or anything. We acquired two dogs but they never paid any attention. It went on for a year or so but we were never frightened, until we had one particular lodger.

He was supposed to be an artist but he spent all his time lounging about. He didn't get up until one o'clock in the afternoon. He had just divorced his wife and we took him in because he had nowhere to live. He was very uncomfortable here, he was quite spooked by these footsteps. At one time he wouldn't sleep upstairs. He said that he kept seeing something come up the stairs and he told us that a dark shape came into his room and stood over him. Some nights he refused to go to bed and stayed in the lounge all night.

The artist was staying with us in the October when we had a terrible week. The whole atmosphere of the house became very disturbed. The footsteps got faster and were very noisy, like someone running up the stairs. Then whatever-it-was came into our room at the top of the house over and over again and bashed the bed. It would crash into the corner of the bed with such force that it would wake up Sarah and myself. This happened three or four times a night for a whole week. We were nervous wrecks. My mother told me to shout at it, and there I was in the middle of the night, running round yelling 'For God's sake, will you b..... off!'. After that it did quieten down. Then, when the artist left, the disturbances faded away.

I did think this might be Captain Emmott protesting at my transfer to the Yeomanry Signal Squadron at Stratford-on-Avon. He had been adjutant to the Worcestershire Yeomanry whose direct descendent is the Yeomanry Squadron in Stourbridge. Indeed, as a Cavalry man, he would have considered that 'the Signals' was no place for a gentleman!

Tardebigge was in Staffordshire in Saxon times, in 1266 the boundaries were changed so that one end of the church was in Worcestershire and the other half in Warwickshire. It was not acquired by Worcestershire until the middle of the 1800s. Although Tardebigge has a church and a public house, in actual fact there is no such place, for Tardebigge is a parish, not a piece of ground. For example, if you are in Bentley, you are then in the parish of Tardebigge, and if you are in Hewell Grange you are also in Tardebigge.

Imprisoned with an Apparition

The story of Hewell Grange has been told many times, how Henry VIII had designs on Lord Windsor's comfortable castle at Stanwell and insisted upon exchanging Bordesley Abbey and its estates for Lord Windsor's residence. Lord Windsor arrived at Bordesley Abbey with his retinue one cold and wet November afternoon and found it ruinous, so moved into one of its lodges, which was Hewell Grange.

The old Hewell Grange before 1895.

Hewell Grange after 1895. Courtesy Phillip Coventry.

When Henry VIII established the Church of England, many wealthy families refused to convert to the new religion and remained in the Roman Catholic faith. Among them were the Windsors of Hewell Grange, together with the Talbots of Grafton, the Winters of Huddington, the Sheldons of Beoley and the Throckmortons of Coughton. It was from these families that the Gunpowder Plot arose, with the result that on 7th November, 1605 a gang of armed and desperate horsemen arrived at Hewell Grange. The gunpowder plot had failed and they were on the run. Lord Windsor had been dead for six months and the new owner was only a boy. The plotters carried away all the gunpowder they could find and it was this same gunpowder that they tried to dry by a fire at Holbeach. The gunpowder exploded, severely burning three of them. The present grange was built in 1884 and has been converted into a Youth Detention centre. There are now three establishments for Her Majesty's guests on the site.

In February 2001, the national press was buzzing with tales of a ghostly monk in Brockhill women's prison. Even the sceptical *Independent on Sunday* reported:

> Inmates and staff at Brockhill women's prison, near Redditch, Worcestershire, are being offered spiritual guidance and support after reports that a ghostly monk has been seen "walking through walls".

Governor Mike Shepherd said:

> At this stage I am not particularly keen to do anything to promote "ghost stories", as I do not think it is helpful for the establishment in general and for some prisoners in particular.

David Shepherd (no relation), who lives on the edge of Hewell Grange, comments:

> The whole area is brimming with ghosts. This house is the old Governor's house and it's on its own in the woods. In my kitchen the television is set into the cupboards. There's a window at the side of these cupboards and several times, while I've been watching the television, out of the corner of my eye, I could see an old lady in a greyish camel coat going past the front of the window. It's been so vivid that I've gone to the front door.
>
> I was doing some voluntary work at a nearby residential home

when I felt a cat rubbing along the back of my legs several times but when I looked down the cat seemed to have run off. I said to the lady who works in the laundry, 'There seems to be a cat here and it won't leave me alone!' Now, this lady could see it, and she said, 'It's a black and white cat, does the name Charlie mean anything to you?'. At the time I said, it didn't, but when I was driving home I suddenly remembered that we had a white on black cat and its name was Charlie.

A young lady who lives on a farm almost opposite Hewell Grange looked out of the window and saw a man in tweeds with a deerstalker hat wandering up the drive to the farm. She rushed out to see what he wanted but he had gone.

A housewife who lives on the edge of the estate in one of the old cottages says that she has a white lady who comes down the stairs at five o'clock every morning. 'She wears a long white dress. She's nothing to be afraid of, she's more frightened of me than I am of her'.

The Flying Hearse

Less than half a mile south from Hewell Grange and Tardebigge is the Foxlydiate Hotel. The Hemming family had been living in the area since 1781, when Sarah Hemming, wife of Richard Hemming, a needle maker, bought three houses at or near Foxlydiate gate. In 1840 Mr W Hemming, decided to build himself a splendid new mansion, Foxlydiate House. On the opposite side of the road was the old Fox and Goose Hotel. Just before World War II, the Fox and Goose was pulled down and the licence transferred to Foxlydiate House.

There's an old story about the Foxlydiate, concerning a Flying Hearse. Sheila Richards writes in *The Rousler* that many years ago there was a quarrel between the vicar and the curate of Studley who were standing in for the vicar of Tardebigge. It was Christmas Eve; the verger of Tardebigge had died and one of them would have to conduct the funeral service on Boxing Day and miss the Boxing Day hunt. In a rage, the vicar killed the curate, borrowed the hearse and horse and buried the curate in the grave meant for the verger. As he passed through Crabbs Cross, Headless Cross and Webheath, he slowed down and hid below the dashboard, but he was spotted by a certain Bill Attewood, a poacher. Bill was found later in a copse with his head caught in a man-trap. The hearse, without the driver, appears on

Christmas Eve when the moon is full. The legend prophecies that those who see it will have passed away within twelve months.

Stories of phantom coaches and horses are relatively common but only rarely do you come across someone who has actually seen one. This story goes back to one September before World War II, when John was eighteen and helping with the threshing at a local farm. Fortunately the coach was not seen at the Foxlydiate with its grim prophecy, but a few miles west, so that John is still with us today to tell the tale:

When the harvest was over they had a party for all the people taking part with plenty of beer. After the party, I started home about one o'clock along this narrow country road, it was only about eight feet wide. I was all on my own. I heard this cart in the distance: a gang of itinerants were living in the area at that time and they were always up to no good, I thought it was them moving, that they had stolen something and were getting away. I could hear this cart coming nearer and nearer. It was only a narrow lane and I thought I was going to get run over so I moved back under a hawthorn hedge. I could hear the clatter of the hooves on the road and the harness creaking and the wheels grinding on the road. It went right past me, I could hear it and feel it but although it was a bright, moonlit night I couldn't see a thing. I was scared then, I ran the one-and-a-half miles home.

I mentioned it to an old neighbour of mine and he said that it was not an uncommon occurrence but he had never come across anybody else who had been so close to it.

Foul Play at Foxlydiate

The Redditch Pictorial Society is dedicated to preserving memorabilia of Old Redditch, and is masterminded by Philip Coventry, who writes:

At the turn of the nineteenth century, that part of south western Redditch known as Foxlydiate was considered to be one of the prettiest spots in Worcestershire. It was also to be the scene of one of the county's most gruesome murders.

Foxlydiate Lane was a peaceful road running north to south linking the main road to Bromsgrove with Webheath on the edge of the Bentley Estate.

Almost within the shadow of Webheath church lay a pair of old semi-detached cottages which belonged to Mrs Cheape, known locally as 'The Squire of Bentley'. In the first cottage lived Mrs Hassel, the widow of a local needle-maker. The other cottage was the home of Mr and Mrs Middleton. Mrs Middleton was originally a paper-maker at Beoley Papermill, her husband, a Bentley man, was a casual farm labourer. The couple had a stormy relationship as Mr Middleton was given to drunken binges during which he treated his wife very badly. He began a drinking session in May 1902 which lasted for two weeks, during which time he was hardly ever sober. As his money ran out he turned to his wife for more funds. Mrs Middleton supplemented their income growing vegetables in their large garden and selling the surplus. Her husband knew that she had just sold the residue of her potato crop and was determined to relieve her of the cash, she was equally determined to hang onto the money.

The matter came to a head on a Friday when neighbours reported violent and persistent quarrelling all through the day and into the evening. Several times Mrs Middleton sought shelter and solace with various of her neighbours, each time returning back to her own home. At around one o'clock Mrs Hassel, whose bedroom was only separated from the Middleton's by a thin dividing wall, was aroused by very loud arguing followed by screaming, after which silence then prevailed. Later, after sleeping fitfully for a while, she awoke again to find her bedroom filling with smoke.

The pair of cottages were well ablaze. Neighbours rushed to save whatever valuables could be rescued and the Redditch Fire Brigade was summoned by Herbert Chambers, the licensee of the Fox and Goose. At the time there was no sign of either of the Middletons. The fire brigade duly arrived but were unable to save either of the properties.

Later the next day, after the fire had been properly doused, they made a grisly discovery. In the back kitchen, where the fire was thought to have started, lay the remains of Mrs Middleton. Her head and limbs had been almost completely burnt away by the severity of the fire. What little of the corpse that remained appeared to be fully dressed, indicating that she had not undressed or prepared for bed. Further evidence at the scene suggested that the fire had been deliberately started by carrying hay from an outside store into the kitchen and setting fire to it.

Mr Middleton had run away but he was found a few days later, convicted of the murder and hanged.

A ghostly hearse is said to fly past the Foxlydiate.

Don't Answer! It's a Ghost!

Michelle once lived in the area:

There are lots of ghost stories about the Foxlydiate. Before I was married I lived in Salters Lane, so I heard all about them. Opposite the Foxlydiate Hotel a path runs into the woods and several people who have walked along there have reported seeing a cape and hat moving through the woods but no body filling them.

When I was about thirteen I saw the white lady of Foxlydiate. There were six of us, three boys and three girls and we were larking about one chilly Autumn evening just as it was getting dusk. By the Salter's Lane Farm the pavement rises above the road, so that there is the road, the bank of grass then the pavement. We were standing there when we saw this lady gliding quite smoothly down the drive of the farm towards us with her hands held out in front of her. I can see her now, I remember it quite vividly. She was about two feet off the ground, with a long white dress and long black hair down to her waist. The dress was slightly shaped but the skirt was straight down and she had long tight sleeves which belled out near the wrists. Then she stopped in the middle of the drive. I said to my friends, 'Can you see that lady coming towards us?' and the others said that they could see her, too. We were not going to hang about, we ran to my house.

As we ran I looked across to the field near my house and she was there! The field is next to the drive to the farm. I said to my dad, 'If anyone knocks at our door, don't answer, it's a ghost'. But my dad always said there were no such things as ghosts, it was imagination.

I was walking through this pathway one night with my husband when I had a strange experience. We were going very slowly because my husband had had an operation and was walking with the aid of sticks. It was dusk and we could both hear men shouting. We said to each other, 'They're having a good row'. As we neared the gate we could hear them more clearly. Someone was pacing off, counting down from ten to zero, then when they reached zero they shouted, 'Turn, Fire!' and we heard two pistol shots. They sound quite different to gunfire. My husband heard them as well, but the fields were quite empty. At the time, we assumed someone was playing a joke.

During the early 1990s I worked in the Foxlydiate as a barmaid. Strange things happened there. It was a job to break those heavy knobbly beer jugs but I have seen one jump off from the back of the shelf and smash on the floor. When refurbishment was taking place, a man's face appeared in the plaster while the workman was plastering. It looked as if someone had pushed their face into the plaster from the other side. The workman was taken aback but he plastered over it and went off to lunch. When he returned the face had reappeared. No matter how many times he plastered over it, it kept returning. He couldn't believe it.

There was a resident ghost by the name of Tom. He was said to be an old coachman. A chef once saw him in the kitchen. She was clearing up – she served until 9.30 pm so it must have been sometime after this – when she saw this man come into the kitchen. She said, 'You can't come in here, have you lost your way?' He looked at her when she spoke but he carried on walking straight across the kitchen and through a wall to the old kitchens upstairs.

Just inside the side entrance door was the bar and by the side of the bar was a door which led up a twisting flight of stairs. You opened the door, went up one step, did a right angle turn and there would be eight steps then another right angle turn and another eight steps to get to the door to the private apartments. On the first landing was a pile of crisp boxes. Usually, one barmaid did the main bar and another the pub bar but you could walk through from one to the other and when we were quiet one person could do both. One night, I was manning both bars when I ran out of crisps. I opened the side door and rushed in, up the first step, round the next bend and there was Tom standing on the next flight. He was in his late 50s with a stocky build, he had a long heavy coat with the old frill on and straight sleeves. He was wearing heavy boots and he had a hat on – I think it was tallish with a brim. I was in too much of a hurry to be bothered by a ghost so I ran up another two steps towards him to get the box of crisps but in that second he disappeared.

The Haunted Highway

In 1992 Yvonne was travelling along the Bromsgrove Highway, her husband was driving:

I'm not into the paranormal but about eight years ago I saw something which I couldn't explain. I don't know whether you would call it a ghost or what.

I was going to a function in Bromsgrove with my husband, it was about seven o'clock in the evening and was just getting dark. We were going along the Bromsgrove Highway and he just about got level with the Foxlydiate Hotel when I saw this lady. She was walking towards Bromsgrove along the grass verge in between the two fast roads. I said to my husband, 'Where on earth is she going?' I was a bit concerned, it was a strange place for a woman to be walking especially when it was just getting dark, and she was quite young. Although she had her back to us I could tell from the way that she was walking that she was in her thirties or early forties. Then I said, 'Whatever she is wearing?'. My husband had a good look so he saw her as well. She had on these old clothes, peasant type, fairly tight, with a long skirt of the kind they used to wear in the eighteenth century. It's difficult to recall the details but I think she was wearing an apron and cloaky-type coat. She had some kind of headgear on, a scarf or a cloth-type bonnet. She was all in grey and white with no distinguishing colour.

We went past, I turned round to take a second look and she had just disappeared. I said, 'Where has she gone?'. I could cope with the fact that she was walking along the centre of the road and the fact that she was wearing strange clothes – I thought she was going to a fancy dress party or something – but not when she completely disappeared. It was only afterwards that I realised that I had seen something that wasn't normal.

Lisa saw something strange a few months ago, still on the Bromsgrove Highway but a little nearer Bromsgrove:

I was driving from Alvechurch to Bromsgrove to see my sister. I had my eleven year old daughter in the car with me. We were going along the road near the exit to Finstall when I noticed a tall thin man in a long brown overcoat and a knitted woollen hat, walking along the grass verge on my left, going the same way as me. It was a very hot day and I turned to my daughter and said, 'I bet that man's feeling hot in that long coat and hat'. She replied, 'What man?'. I looked back and there was no sign of anyone. There were no driveways or gates that he could have turned into and he must have disappeared in the split second that I turned to my daughter.

The Faithful Dog

Finally, a strange story from Finstall village itself:

An elderly friend of mine has recently lost his wife. He has been keeping her ashes in the house but his daughter persuaded him to take them to Tardebigge church and have them scattered. They had a little dog, just a mongrel, and the day before he took the ashes the dog began behaving strangely, which he had never done so before. They scattered the ashes but when they returned, the dog refused to stay in the house and ran off. They found him and brought him home but now he sits in the drive all the time, halfway between the house and the gate, and refuses to go indoors. They wonder if it's anything to do with the ashes.

Cooking up a Haunting at Clent Hills

The Clent Hills are on the edge of the Black Country and ever since the Industrial Revolution they have been the playground of Black Country folk. Many townspeople have chosen to retire here, and several residential homes have been built. Until recently, Karen worked in one of them:

All kinds of strange things happened there and it wasn't an old building, it was new and purpose-built.

I have never seen anything like the things that happened to the cook in the kitchen. Saucepans would suddenly shoot across the work surface for no reason. I was in there once when a saucepan of hard-boiled eggs moved along towards her and then went down her side. The laundry room was next to the kitchen and often the nurses on night duty said that, through one of the glass doors, they had seen a woman walk across the corridor outside but when they went to have a look no-one was there. I think I saw it once although I couldn't swear that it wasn't my own reflection.

One morning, about 8.30, I was at the end where all the bathrooms were and I was running a bath for one of the patients who couldn't walk. The patient was waiting in her bed and I was on my own. I looked up and I saw a woman going past the bathroom door. At first I thought it was the patient who couldn't walk. I thought, 'Blimey, she's been having us all on'. Then I realised that it wasn't her but another patient who had died recently. She was unmistakable because she was not a very nice woman and she used to steal things and scurry back to her room; when I saw her she was scurrying just as she did when she was alive. I saw her quite clearly down to the knees but below her knees there was nothing.

We had a woman in there whose husband had died recently. We often felt there was someone in the bedroom with her. One of the other nurses saw a ghostly figure of a man in her room. She said to the woman, 'Did your husband wear a flat cap and a tweed jacket?' and she went on to describe what she had seen. The woman said, 'Did you know my husband?'

Then there was Flo, who became ill very suddenly and died. When you went into her bedroom just before she died you would feel that someone had gone in with you. Several of the nurses remarked on the fact that a long shadow would stretch out in front of them of a second person who wasn't there.

... and Barnt Green

Another cook who 'brewed a haunting' comes from the 1914 edition of the *Journal of the British Society for Psychical Research*. In line with the Society's custom, pseudonyms or initials were used for all the persons involved and the place was only named as 'a haunted house in Worcestershire'. However, it was set back from the road, surrounded

The Clent Hills.

by beautiful gardens and not far from a railway station. Looking at old maps, we assume that it could have been in the Barnt Green area, on the edge of the Lickey Hills.

In 1914, Sir William Barrett, a distinguished Edwardian psychical researcher, received a letter from a Mrs Roberts, asking if he would visit her in an attempt to bring to an end 'the terror besieging her household'.

Sir William stayed in the house for a few days but unfortunately heard nothing. He interviewed each member of the family in turn and after his departure Mrs Roberts kept him in touch with events by letter.

The whole bizarre episode had begun at 8 pm one Sunday evening, when the housemaid, Annie, heard a noise like a dog moaning coming from under her employer's bed. Then an invisible hand pushed her backwards against the dressing table and she saw a figure materialise, tall and clothed in white, apparently from under the bed and disappear through the door. She heard its footsteps on the landing.

The cook, Ethel, reluctantly confessed that she had heard groaning and strange noises and once, when she heard a stampede of footsteps, she had lit a candle but nothing was to be seen. Sometimes her bedclothes had been whipped off. Another servant, Violet, said that she had heard the window of the day nursery being thrown open then slammed down again, followed by sounds of furniture being knocked about. A few weeks later, she had heard the tramping of such heavy footsteps coming into the room that her bed shook. These steps had walked across to the dressing table. On another occasion a hand had gripped her throat so hard that it hurt. Suspecting an intruder, Mr Roberts had fitted up an electric bell so that Violet could summon him each time something happened; each time he rushed to her room but nothing could be found.

Mrs Roberts herself was involved in a disturbance. She was eating her dinner at 9 pm after spending the day nursing her husband (who had been taken ill) when Violet rushed in to say that terrible noises were coming from the larder. By the time Mrs Roberts reached the larder the noises had stopped so she returned to her meal, but a temporary maid then rushed in to say that the noises were continuing in the cellar. Mrs Roberts then had to attend to her husband, but the maid later told her that footsteps had slowly mounted the cellar stairs towards her. She had shouted, 'What do you want?' and the footsteps had stopped.

A few nights later, the parlour maid, Rose, had awoken at about 3 am to find, silhouetted against the window, a form 'darker than night'. She could make out that he had protruding ears. Anne (the housemaid) was sound asleep in the next bed but did not stir. Rose had hidden under the bedclothes and when she finally peeped out, the apparition had disappeared.

Sir William discovered that Ethel, the cook (an elderly woman), had experienced strange manifestations such as footsteps, moving furniture and smashing crockery in her previous place of employment. He suspected that the haunting was poltergeist activity, this time centring round, not the customary teenager, but the elderly cook!

In August of that year, Sir William received a letter from Mrs Roberts telling him that the cook had left the household and that the paranormal phenomena had disappeared.

The Poplars Apparition

We shall never know the identity of the haunted house but the Old Poplars at Barnt Green answered to the description and had the reputation of being haunted. It has now been demolished and a new estate has been built on the site, which includes Poplar Drive. Richard lived in the new estate until recently and he says:

> I did actually see something paranormal. I woke up in the middle of the night to see this apparition standing at the foot of my bed. It was like a human-shaped mist, whitey-grey and shimmering. I thought I must be dreaming so I closed my eyes and opened them and it was still there. It seemed quite benign and friendly. I assumed it was something to do with my aunty who was very ill with cancer in the Queen Elizabeth Hospital. The next night she died.
>
> A few days later, the night before she was due to be buried, the same thing happened again. This time I could see the form more clearly and it seemed to be a female. The veil was hiding her features but it gradually began to fall away, starting from the top of her head, so that I was beginning to see her features. At this point I turned the light on and the apparition went.
>
> That same night, it rained heavily and the grave in which she was to be buried caved in, so that they couldn't bury her the following day.

More of the Headless Horseman (Lickey Hills)

In Haunted Worcestershire, a retired engineer living on the Lickey Hills tells how he heard the sound of horses' hooves in his garden one evening and when he went to investigate, saw a headless horseman disappearing through his hedge. This was thought by local people to be Brady, a notorious highwayman hanged at Worcester in 1806.

However, David Evans, who lives in Bournville, remarks that it is much more likely to be Captain Jamie Hind, as highwaymen were only hung whereas Hind was convicted of high treason as well as highway robbery which meant that in 1652 he was hung, drawn and quartered. David explains:

> Hind was an ardent Royalist who fought as a captain in the civil war of 1641-1646 and, as a highwayman, he preyed only on Round-heads. He is thought to have helped Charles Stuart (later Charles II) to escape. After the civil war he was captured, pardoned as a highwayman under the Act of Oblivion but interrogated before the House of Commons regarding the King's escape. He was convicted of high treason and hanged, drawn and quartered, with his head placed on Worcester Bridge gate. All this is authentic history but now we come to speculation. The head was taken away by Royalists and buried in a churchyard in Worcester, but we don't know which churchyard. His torso could have been wired up, tarred and put on the gibbet at Lickey as he helped the King to escape in Worcestershire. He was the only highwayman to lose his head.

Hind is remembered as the archetype of the 'gentleman thief', a contemporary poem described him as follows:

He made our wealth one common store,
he robbed the rich to feed the poor:
what did immortal Caesar more?

If in due light his deeds we scan
as Nature points us out the plan,
hanged was an honourable man!

Honour, the virtue of the brave,
to Hind that turn of genius gave
which made him scorn to be a slave.

James Hind, from an old woodcut of 1652.

DROITWICH AREA

rom prehistoric times until the early 1900s, Droitwich was the great salt town of England and no expense was spared when building or rebuilding its churches. Saint Andrew's, on the corner of the High Street, has a fine thirteenth century chancel arch and north tower. The impressive tower of Saint Augustine's at Dodderhill stands high over the town and was rebuilt in 1708 to replace one destroyed during the civil war. Parts of Saint Peter's, south of the centre, are 800 years old. It contains some medieval stained glass, fifteenth century tiles, and a sixteenth century handsome, low-pitched roof. On the southern outskirts of the town, the Roman Catholic church of the Sacred Heart and Saint Catherine is a tourist attraction, the inside glittering with mosaics on every surface.

Yet Droitwich has lost at least two churches. There was once a chapel on the bridge over the Salwarpe, through the centre of which passed the main road to Bromsgrove. The reading desk was on one side of the road and the congregation on the other. Vehicles made a detour but foot passengers were allowed through. The bridge is still known locally as Chapel Bridge. Friary Street is named after an Au-

View of the salt works towards the end of the 1800s.

gustinian Friary built there in 1331 and near to the Friary was the church of Saint Nicholas. During the civil war, the Royalists kept a large quantity of ammunition in the church so the parliamentarians brought a cannon to the higher ground at Dodderhill and fired at the Church, totally destroying it. Three church windows were rescued by villagers and incorporated into the rebuilding of the Old Cock Inn.

Friary Street continues into the High Street. John Leland, wrote in the sixteenth century that the town itself 'is somewhat foule and dirtye (when any rain falleth), with much carriage through the streets being ill-paved or not paved'. Droitwich was once a wretched place in which to live, smoke and vapour was continually ascending from salt furnaces and pans. However, the High Street is now a delightful assortment of tiny and unusual shops, such as the antiquarian book shop, a fire shop (selling fire surrounds, brass brushes and shovels etc) and the Ickle Gift Shop.

The Ickle Haunting

In the late summer of 2000, the two Burgess sisters, Rachel and Sarah, both found themselves unemployed. Sarah had been working in London and her job came to an end, while Rachel had just returned from a tour of Europe. Rachel explains:

> We sat down and asked ourselves what we could do – something that we could do together. We had always wanted to open a gift shop and we thought that this was our opportunity. We decided to sell hand-made craft gifts. As we lived in Droitwich, premises in the High Street would be only just round the corner.

> We had a choice of two properties and chose one in the High Street on the corner of Gurneys Lane. I think this building is one of the oldest in Droitwich. Next door is a Fire Shop and they tell me that, at one time, our shop was part of their premises. The adjoining door has now been blocked off. As well as being part of next door's shop, we were also the living quarters and divided into three tiny rooms with

a little window overlooking the street. Next door, in one of the upstairs rooms, they have a chimney breast with the marks of swords and bayonets from the Civil War of 1642-1646 so the premises must have been built before then.

We made a list of what we would like to sell and chose the name, 'The Ickle Gift Shop'. We opened on 8th September 2000. We thought there was something strange as soon as we first moved in. The Visa card machine seemed to have a mind of its own. It would beep twice, then you would put the card in and it would beep and say that the card had been rejected and there it was still in the machine. The next morning, all by itself, it ran off a list of all the cardholders. We rang up the company who owned it and asked if they had ordered the printout for us, but they said they couldn't do that from their end. Sometimes the machine would beep and we hadn't even put a card in.

The back room was very cold, so was this room, but we blamed it on the winter weather. We brought more heating in but it didn't seem to make any difference. My sister, Sarah, felt that someone was behind her two or three times when she was standing behind the counter. She could sense that someone was there and it gave her a cold shiver up her spine. She didn't like to be in the shop on her own when it was closed, especially when it was winter and dark outside.

The ghost of Emma Vernon roams these fields round Hanbury.

The local newspaper offices are just over the road and they heard about our ghost and gave us a write-up about it. A paranormal expert saw it in the papers and called in. We took him upstairs, where there are two unused rooms, and he said that he could see a lady in a big straw hat and a flowing, long-sleeved gown. He said that she was a nice lady, he had spoken to her and she said that she was there because she was worried about us. He asked her not to stay here. He told us that if we were stressed, she would come round more. We had been very stressed, it's difficult setting up your own business and at times my sister had been quite emotional.

After his visit the shop seemed much warmer and we haven't had any more problems, except for last week. One very hot day, when there was no wind, I was standing near the open doorway and the door closed very slowly and carefully.

Roman Remains

Sometime between 47 and 70 AD the Romans arrived at Droitwich. They built a fort at Dodderhill, and a large villa complex to the west of the fort, where the industrial estates now stand. In *Unquiet Spirits of Worcestershire* Robert Nicklin tells the story of a Roman soldier who appeared in a factory on the Berryhill Industrial Estate. George was working on the same estate for 38 years and he says that it is definitely haunted.

> With my own eyes I have seen a tin which had been left on the table lift itself up and fly across the table. When I was on nights I could hear strange clanking noises, like the clanking of chains. Doors slowly opened and closed of their own accord. I would see a light on and think, I'll go round later and switch that light off but when I reached the place where the light was on, it would be off.
>
> A mate of mine went to work in the factory at 3.30 am. When the day shift arrived at six o'clock the next morning, he was standing outside the building shivering and shaking like a jelly. He would never tell anyone what he saw and he refused to go on nights again. There are ghosts there, there's no doubt about it.

Emma Vernon Walks Again (Hanbury)

Emma Vernon was the great-granddaughter of Sir Thomas Vernon who built Hanbury Hall in 1710. She was born at Hanbury Hall in the middle of the eighteenth century. After three years of marriage to a member of the distinguished Cecil family, she eloped with the local curate. Her ghost is so well-known that the local pub has been packed with people hoping to catch a glimpse of her. Josie is one of the many to have seen her:

> My brother lives in Hanbury and I visit him occasionally in the evening. When I leave him he always says, 'Drive carefully, lock your car doors and don't give anybody a lift'. Late one evening after visiting him, probably somewhere near midnight, I drove carefully from the direction of the Vernon Arms through Hanbury woods. I was just nearing the end of the woods when my headlights picked up this youngish girl on the right hand side of the road, all in black except for a white

circular area below the waist which I took to be a pinafore. I thought 'What's a young girl doing out at this time of night and especially in a pinafore?'. Then I said to myself, 'I hope she's not going to do anything silly and run across the road in front of me' so I put the brake on to slow right down. I didn't stop because I assumed she had someone with her who wasn't visible because of the bushes. At that point I was level with her and suddenly she disappeared. I thought, 'Where has she gone?'

The next time I went past that same spot in daylight I looked to see if there was a gate or a hole in the hedge that she could have got through to disappear so suddenly but no, it was a thick bramble hedge.

At that time I didn't know anything about the ghost of Emma Vernon. It was not until some months later that I went for a walk on Sunday afternoon with my brother and his wife up to Hanbury Church and on the way back to their house they were talking about the story of Emma Vernon. I said to them 'I have seen her!'.

This is the only time I have ever seen anything like that. I kept it to myself, I didn't tell anyone. I'm really a person who doesn't believe in this sort of thing but I definitely saw someone there that night and she definitely disappeared.

At Dead of Night (Holt)

Holt is really three villages, the old village centred round the church and castle, the modern village, and the riverside resort of Holt Fleet.

Holt Castle.

In the twelfth century, a team of stonemasons at Leominster blossomed into one of the great English schools of sculpture, working at churches across Worcestershire and the neighbouring counties. It combined features from across the world – the Far East, Ireland, France and Scandinavia – with English traditions to produce carvings full of vitality and feeling.

Parts of the beautiful church at Holt, especially the font, are thought to be examples of their work. The entrance to the churchyard faces the castle front, and both once stood in the middle of a forest. The tower of the castle is fourteenth century and parts of the hall date back to the fifteenth. For generations it was the home of the powerful Beauchamp family. In the final years of the fourteenth century John Beauchamp became a favourite of Richard II and was made Lord de Beauchamp, Baron of Kidderminster but not long after he received the title he was beheaded on Tower Hill in London. The monks of Worcester Cathedral claimed his body. Later Holt Castle became the home of the Bromleys, Sir Thomas Bromley was the Lord High Chancellor who condemned Mary Queen of Scots to death and his son, Sir Henry Bromley, tracked down four of the gunpowder plotters at Hindlip Hall.

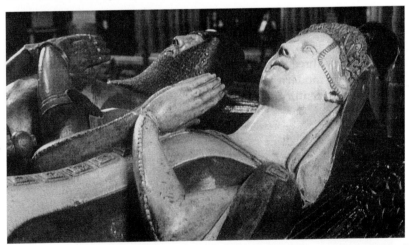

Effigy of Lord and Lady Beauchamp in Worcester Cathedral Lord Beauchamp was beheaded on Tower Hill and his body was claimed by the monks of Worcester Cathedral.

Isaac Wedley, writing at the turn of the century, remarks, 'of course the place is haunted' and continues:

Two generations ago it was religiously believed by the servants at the castle that a mysterious lady in black promenaded at dead of night, a certain passage near to the attics, and that the cellar had likewise been occupied by some unearthly bird, resembling a raven, who would extinguish the visitor's candle with a horrid flapping of wings, and leave the affrighted wretch with scarce strength enough to take back his shaking limbs.

He quotes a poem of which the second verse reads:

> Where men are locked in slumber
> The rustling sounds are heard
> Of dainty ladies' dresses
> Of laughs and whispered word;
> Of waving wind of feathers
> And steps of dancing feet,
> In the garrets of Holt Castle
> When the winds of winter beat.

Affrighting the Domestics (Salwarpe)

Salwarpe lies on the A38 as it encircles Droitwich and is one of Worcestershire's undiscovered beauty spots. The *Worcestershire Village Book* published by the Worcestershire Federation of Women's Institutes, reads:

> For the imaginative, there are certainly ghosts in Salwarpe. When the mists swirl over the weir surely a carriage passed from distant High Park, over the river, to the church? A clatter of horses' hooves down the land and one expects to see a company of Yorkists, with swirling cloaks, rendezvousing at the Court. In the moonlight, among the quiet churchyard paths, one can imagine the whispering figures of monks, patiently pacing to and fro.

According to John Noake, who was writing in the first half of the nineteenth century:

> On the other side of the canal (to the church) is an ancient timber structure, said to have been formerly the mansion-house, until the construction of the canal pared off a slice of it. In revenge for this act of

mutilation the ghost of a former occupier occasionally revisits his old haunts, affrights Mr Quarrell's domestics, and may be seen on peculiarly dark nights, with deprecatory aspect, to glide down the embankment and suicidally commit himself to the waters below.

He adds that, on the right hand side of the pathway going towards the church, was an old red sandstone tomb.

Some years ago the late Mr Gresley had it opened. He found therein the skeleton of a very large man, the skull lying on one side of it, as though the man was beheaded.

Perhaps the historians of Worcestershire will come forward with some suggestions as to who this could be.

Salwarpe, where a figure glides into the water on dark night.

EVESHAM AREA

vesham has two beautiful parish churches side by side, All Saints' and Saint Lawrence's. No-one is certain why, perhaps one was for the townsfolk and the other for the pilgrims who visited the tomb of Saint Egwin. South of these two churches was once a magnificent priory, founded by the Saint in 714 but demolished in the purges of Henry VIII. All that is left now, apart from the Almonry, is a wall and an archway, its weathered carving giving us a glimpse of the splendid ornamentation which once existed.

One of Evesham's pride and joys is the beautiful Bell Tower. It should, in fact, not be here at all as it was built at a time when Henry VIII was poised to take over the Church and the suppression of the monasteries was in the air. While other religious institutions were reducing their assets, Abbot Clement Lichfield embarked on a huge construction programme. He built a grammar school which is now the Working Men's Club. He built a chantry to his namesake (Saint Clement) in Saint Lawrence's and a chapel to house his own mortal remains in All Saints'.

He also built the 110 feet (33.52 metres) high Bell Tower. When the news of suppression came, he wrote a desperate letter to the King, asking him to save the priory, then when this was ignored, he could not bear to surrender it and appointed a young monk as abbot in his place. Sad and disillusioned, he retired to his grange at Offenham.

As long as anyone can remember, the Bell Tower has had the reputation of being haunted. Local people who pass by say that cold shivers run up their spine or something seems not quite right. A few years ago the Bell Tower was being repaired by workmen from outside Evesham so they had not been told any stories about the Bell Tower being haunted. The Warden, whose job it was to check up on the work, went to have a chat with the Foreman. The Foreman said that he had seen a ghost in there and wasn't too happy about going back inside.

Simon de Montfort, from the windows of Chartres Cathedral.

Evesham Bell Tower at the beginning of the 1900s.
Courtesy Phillip Coventry.

Big Bells and Little Belles

Olive, who now lives in Droitwich, is eighty and she says that the next incident happened when she was fourteen or fifteen:

> My sister and I had been to the cinema at Bengeworth and were returning to our home on other side of the town. It was about 10.30 on a bright, moonlit night in midsummer and we were taking a short cut through the Bell Tower fields. When we neared the Bell Tower, we could see that two monks were walking about seven yards in front of us. They looked quite normal and we didn't take much notice of them as we walked across the grass. Their cloaks were grey and they were grey-haired, their hoods were not over their heads but down their backs. Their heads were bent and they were obviously talking as they kept looking at each other. Then they walked straight through the tombstones which were there then – I think they've gone now. There used to be a door into the Bell Tower that was kept locked – they walked straight through that as well. My sister and I looked at each other with our mouths open.
>
> Two or three days later, when we were once again walking under the Bell Tower, my sister and I realised that the two monks had actually walked through a solid stone wall.
>
> There were two of us and we both saw them. I still can't believe it. We were both young teenagers, too young to go into a pub so we hadn't been drinking or anything. We still talk about it now.

The Battle for Democracy

Evesham is well-known as the site of the battle of Evesham, for it was here, in the loop of the river, that Simon de Montfort, his son and his army were massacred. We are told that as he fell, dark clouds covered the sun so that the monks could not see to read the psalms. The battle only lasted three hours but when it was over more than four thousand soldiers lay dead and dying. Although Simon de Montfort died, his vision of a parliament co-operating with the King, lived on.

The body of Earl Simon was hacked to pieces and the head and hands were sent to Lady Mortimer at Wigmore as a trophy. In *Historic Worcestershire* by W Salt Brassington, we read that:

...the messenger, on his arrival at Wigmore Castle, found the lady attending mass at the neighbouring abbey; he entered the church, and as he told Lady Mortimer the news, the priest was elevating the host. At that solemn moment, the hands of Earl Simon were seen to clasp themselves in prayer above the messenger's head, though they were afterwards found in the bag sewn up as before. Lady Mortimer was so alarmed at this occurrence that she sent the hands back to Evesham.

The monks of Evesham gathered the other remains together and buried them in their church, de Montfort's tomb soon became celebrated for the miracles wrought there.

His remains now lie in a marked grave in the park behind the two churches.

Friends and Enemies

During the last half of the seventeenth century, Evesham was notorious for another reason – for its terrible persecution of the Society of Friends. They were popularly known as Quakers because some of them trembled with emotion when they spoke.

The first meetings of the Friends were held in Bengeworth, on the eastern side of the town, and converts were usually small shopkeepers, such as butchers and cobblers, and labourers. Their aim was not to start a new sect, but to bring the whole of the Christian Church back from 'the dark days of apostasy', a philosophy which was not popular with the local clergy. In 1655 George Hopkins, vicar of Evesham, preached such a tirade against the Quakers that the congregation marched to Bengeworth and surrounded their meeting house. The Friends remained calm and the crowd dispersed. From then on, the Friends were arrested, fined heavily, whipped, beaten and kept in a dark, filthy prison on starvation rations for periods varying from overnight to months on end. Visitors were locked in with them overnight and had to pay to be released. The Friends tried to mount a vigil outside the prison but eight armed men were paid to keep them away.

The persecutions even reached the ears of Oliver Cromwell, who was sympathetic towards the dissidents. He ordered the magistrate to repay their fines. The magistrate did so, but confiscated goods instead. Oliver Cromwell ordered him to return them.

Fourteen Quakers were arrested in the autumn of 1655 because of legislation forbidding a meeting of more than eight people. Three of them were incarcerated for fourteen weeks in a dungeon below the main prison. Later they appeared to have been joined by others. The dungeon was twelve feet square, without light, air or sanitation. Starvation rations were passed through a hole fourteen inches wide, and the mayor had a trapdoor made through which he removed all their bedding. It stank so much that people in the street could not bear to stand by the hole leading to it. Those who became sick and ill were thrown out into the cold, dark night. When the days became hot, some prisoners lay for several days almost without breathing, 'like men asleep'. The wife of one of the Friends asked if she could remove the excrement, but she was put in the stocks for asking. Two women went to visit and were placed in stocks over the dungeon for 15 hours. They were released into the freezing night, one of them died shortly afterwards.

When Oliver Cromwell died and Charles II came to the throne a wave of hostility swept through the whole nation against all dissenters. Between 1661 and 1669, 13,562 Quakers were imprisoned throughout England. In Evesham, the Baptists and Presbyterians met secretly but the Friends insisted on making their views known openly. They publicly announced their services, preached in the open and harangued the vicar after services. Atrocities therefore continued. For example, in 1662 soldiers arrived, rounded up the Quakers and ordered them to appear at Worcester the next day. Then they were all released except for sixty year old Richard Walker, a poor sickly man. The soldiers drove him on foot before the horses and when he collapsed, they dragged

Evesham High Street in about 1910. Courtesy Phillip Coventry.

PriceLess Shoes stands on the site of the old dungeon.

him by force. The Major beat him down with his horse and threatened to shoot him. He was taken to Worcester gaol but died soon afterwards.

Despite fierce persecution, the number of nonconformists grew until, in 1672, Charles had to admit that the policy of oppression had failed. When William and Mary came to the throne in 1688 a Toleration Act was passed which helped the Friends but they were not completely accepted until the late 1800s.

The site of the prison and the dungeon where these atrocities took place was in the High Street, by the Old Town Hall, in the premises now occupied by PriceLess Shoes. Below the shop is a cellar and in recent years another cellar has been discovered below the first one.

The locals say that there have been 'strange goings-on' in those premises for years. Kim had been working in PriceLess Shoes for twelve months when she reported:

> It all started for me the day before Christmas Eve 1999. My boss phoned me up and said she was phoning from the shop. I said, 'Why, what's up?' because we had been working there until seven or eight the night before, putting the sale posters up. She said that the alarms kept going off and the police thought it might be caused by the movement of the posters in the draughts so we had to take them all down. Anyway, she took them down but the alarms still kept going off. We didn't alarm the premises over the Christmas holiday, the police said that they would keep an eye on the shop.

The security firm which services the alarms came out and they told us that the movement setting off the alarms came from the middle stock room upstairs. We went up but nothing was there except for loads of dead flies. The strange thing is that there are no doors in or out of the middle stock room. You have to go through the main store and right round to get to it, then the door is locked and only my boss and I have the keys.

The alarms have a control point which bleeps. My children came home and said, 'The alarm's going off'. I told them that was impossible, they were switched off. They said, 'It's not the main burglar alarm, but the little tagging system'. I went to have a look and sure enough, although it was turned off it was still bleeping away.

My boss and I have heard footsteps overhead, coming from the stock room, when we know that we were the only ones on the premises. They started at Christmas time and went on through January. The first time we heard them we looked at each other in disbelief. We said, 'It didn't happen, we didn't hear it'.

Other strange things have happened. Boxes have been thrown about and items left in one place have turned up in another. My mobile telephone rang from PriceLess but nobody was there.

On Boxing night my family always goes to the Working Men's Club. We passed the store on our way and we happened to notice the stepladders in the window. On the way home, the children noticed that the ladders had mysteriously moved themselves to a window on the other side of the shop and were in the opposite window. This really freaked them out.

There used to be a hairdressers next door which was on a level with the stock room and they told me that they had been haunted for many years. The father of the hairdresser who owned the shop had seen the ghost, he said that it was a butcher. We call our ghost Casper but they called theirs Fred.

It's very appropriate that Evesham should find a haunted shoe shop in its centre. The town was fined 1,000 pairs of shoes by King Charles for assisting the Parliamentary army across the River Avon.

Too Many Guests

On the south-west borders of Evesham, a young professional couple live in a half-timbered cottage. One of the bedrooms had been divided into two, so in 1998 they removed the adjoining wall and made it into one again. The wife says:

About a month later odd things began to happen in the room in which I kept my clothes, which was different to my bedroom. Once, the window flew off its hinges when there was no wind. We had laid a new carpet and a large, dark, blood-red stain appeared on it. Sometimes the cat from next door would go up quite happily but at other times, he arched his back and he'd be gone.

This was our guest room and five of our guests saw something strange in there. One friend had come over from America and as she was suffering from jet lag, she said, 'I will have a lie down before lunch'. She was downstairs again half an hour later. She said there was a little woman dressed in white sitting at the end of her bed. We all attributed this to jet lag.

An acquaintance of ours came to stay. We didn't know him very well but we said that he could stay with us for two weeks while he looked for a house. Later, at breakfast, he told us that at 3.30 in the morning a woman had walked through his bedroom. I said, 'Well, it wasn't me' and he said, 'I know, she was in white'.

Another friend came and she was looking in the mirror when she saw a white figure behind her but when she turned round nobody was there. Yet another friend stayed in that room when my husband and I were on holiday. We have an old sword hanging on the wall downstairs and he ended up taking it to bed with him. He said, 'I know it was stupid but it made me feel better'. He didn't tell us that until later.

For about twelve months every time I took a dress out of my wardrobe (I always wear dresses) it had a little cut in the same place on the right hip. We looked for all kinds of reasonable causes. Perhaps it was something in the car. I have a special car seat for my back and we put plasters over the rivets, it still kept going on. I had even changed the car. Then one day I came home and one of the dresses that I haven't worn for a long time was just sticking out of the wardrobe and it had got a cut all down the one side.

A friend of ours said, 'Why don't you have a paranormal expert to look into it?'. A lady came out and said she could see three ghosts in the house. One was a religious figure and he was standing with a book under his arm and, although he didn't live here, he was booking people in. He had brought a servant with him, however there was already a servant in the house dressed in white and holding a pair of scissors. When the other servant arrived she was jealous and cut my clothes. The paranormal expert actually spoke to the servant, she said, 'This lady doesn't mind you living here but you are not to damage her clothes'.

What the expert didn't know is that our house was once used as a staging post by coach loads of pilgrims on their way to Evesham Abbey. Ever since then the clothes have not been cut and the strange thing is the stain on the carpet has got lighter until it has almost disappeared. From that day on we have never had anything odd happen.

A Monk at the Window (Offenham)

There's an old legend that Offa the Terrible had a palace here, hence its name. This could be true as Offa was well known in the Severn Valley, however, Offenham could have received a charter in 709 whereas, apparently, Offa was not born until a few decades later. However, hopefully, one day a tractor or a digger will uncover evidence of a large Saxon building.

Offa's father was the deputy governor of the huge Midland kingdom of Mercia, but he was driven out by the King. The reason, is it said, why Offa was not killed was that he was weak, blind, deaf, dumb and lame. Then suddenly, his limbs straightened, his eyes opened, he began to speak and he became a great warrior. He fought the King who had driven out his father and won, eventually becoming King of all England except Northumbria.

The mention of his name brought such fear to his enemies that Mercia enjoyed a period

Gargoyles on Offenham Church Tower.

Offenham High Street, showing the maypole at the far end.

of peace throughout his reign. In those days the Welsh regularly raided the Midlands, and so Offa built a dyke to keep them out which went from somewhere near Prestatyn in North Wales down to the Severn estuary.

In the seventh century Offenham and the surrounding villages were given to Evesham Abbey, and Offenham became the administrative centre. The Abbots created a deer park here in the twelfth century, encircled by a wide ditch and bank, and over the next two centuries built and enlarged a residence on the site of Court Farm. It probably had a stone hall, stables, farm buildings, and a nearby fish pond. It was here that the last abbot of Evesham, Clement Lichfield, spent his last days after Henry VIII closed the abbey in 1540. Ghostly monks have often been seen wandering about the village. Early one morning, in one of the newer houses, a lady woke up and saw a man standing on the other side of her bedroom window. At first she thought the window cleaner had arrived and said to herself, 'He's starting cleaning the windows early'. But then she realised it couldn't be the window cleaner because he was wearing a monk's habit.

Visiting Offenham today, it seems unbelievable that until the seventeenth century, one of the main roads to London passed through the village, and across a nearby ford. Main Street is happily rooted in the fifteenth and sixteenth centuries, with many ancient and half-timbered houses. On the east side six cottages have one long single thatched roof, the second longest continuous thatch in England.

Maypoles and Grey Ladies

The Main Street ends, surprisingly, with one of the tallest maypoles in England. Eighty feet high, it has red, white and blue stripes and is topped by a weathercock. The Maypole is still used for the May Day festivities which go back (with interruptions) to at least the fourteenth century, perhaps even before Offa's time. They could have been a survival of the Celtic festival of Beltain, which celebrated the arrival of summer. Among the various rituals and ceremonies symbolising the fertilising powers of nature was one of dancing round the Maypole. This was originally made from white hawthorn, which represented the transition into summer, but the custom was replaced by garlanded poles and the Offenham one is made from Larch. Oliver Cromwell banned the May Day festivities, but the ban was lifted when Charles II came to the throne. In gratitude, the May Day celebrations were moved to May 29th, which is Charles II's birthday and the day that he returned to London. The May Day celebrations at Offenham last for a week, and include stalls in the Main Street, dancing round the Maypole, a treasure hunt, a fancy dress competition, a disco and children's sports.

Bruce Watson, in his *Offenham Village and Maypole* writes that there is a tradition that, after the battle of Evesham in 1265, cavalry and soldiers from Simon de Montfort's defeated army fled from the battlefield and tried to cross the river at the ford but they were chased by the royalists and massacred. The promontory on the opposite side of the river is known as 'Dead Men's Ait', and bones of men and horses have been found in the river during dredging.

The older villagers say that several of the old houses have ghosts. The lady in the following story moved to the village about forty years ago:

> My husband saw it first. He couldn't sleep one night and he was lying awake when in the darkness he could make out the shape of a female moving slowly and gracefully from the wall on one side of the bedroom across the room to the wall on the other side. He thought it was me in a long nightdress with full sleeves and said to himself, 'Why doesn't she put the light on?'. Then he saw that I was fast asleep in bed next to him. He was a bit startled but he didn't mind. We decided afterwards that she must have been friendly.

This was some time in 1995, and about six months later, when I was in the house on my own, I went into our bedroom without bothering to put the light on. There she was! It looked as if she was standing on our bed. She was a grey, see-through shape, I could tell that she was quite young as her posture was very upright but I couldn't see her clearly enough to say whether she had long hair or short hair or anything like that. She startled me. I said, 'Oh my goodness!' but she didn't frighten me or anything like that. Although our house is an old cottage with a long and interesting history, we never thought anything of it, we didn't expect anything to appear in our house. It wasn't as though we were waiting to see it.

We haven't seen her since but a strange thing is that, although I have never mentioned anything about the ghost, my granddaughter refuses to sleep in any bedroom except one and then she will only sleep on a certain side of the bed. She says she can feel that something is there.

One reason I wasn't frightened was because this was the second ghost I had seen, so I had grown used to the idea. A few years before that, I was walking down the High Street in the dark late one evening and I was almost at the end of the road when a quivering, shimmering shape came out of the wall and hovered in front of me, then it went back into the wall again. I couldn't tell whether it was a man or a woman. It was a human shape but quite tall as its feet didn't go down to the floor.

KIDDERMINSTER AREA

 paragraph in Nash's Worcestershire reveals a horrifying story:

'Four persons were accused of witchcraft and brought to Kidderminster gaol in May 1660. One widow Robinson, her two daughters and a man. The daughter was accused of saying that the King should not live long and he will die and he would suffer from ill-health. First they were put to ducking in the river but they would not sink but swam aloft. The man had five teats, the woman three and the eldest daughter one.'

In fact the king, Charles II, who had just returned from exile to be crowned, lived for another 25 years.

The early Roman Catholic Church considered any beliefs other than the authorised teaching of the Christian church to be heresy. In 1258, witchcraft was said to be a heresy and the great witch-hunt began. For five hundred years, the deformed, the old, the ugly, the psychics, the unpopular, the herbalists were hunted and tortured. Heaven help anyone who was born with a deformity such as six fingers and toes or an unusual number of nipples, as in the case above.

In medieval times a common belief was that disease or any disaster was caused by the evil eye. The family concerned would look around for anyone likely to have cursed the sufferer. It only needed one accuser for someone to be put on trial for being a witch. The unlucky woman would have most of her clothes removed, her thumbs were tied to the opposite big toes and a rope would be tied round her waist before she was thrown far into the pond. If she floated, she was judged to be a witch and rejected by the water, if she sank, she was innocent but by the time her innocence had been established it was usually too late. If she survived the water ordeal, a 'witches mark' was looked for, a blemish on the skin which, when pierced, did not bleed, and the third phase was a confession. In England, physical violence was not allowed and so confessions were forced by starving or keeping the victim awake. After hanging, a witch was usually buried at crossroads with a stake through her heart.

There are many references to the persecution of witches in various towns and villages. Somewhere near the crossroads at Powick lies the body of Mistress Hicks, who brought 'the blight' to plants and animals.

In 1649, in Worcester, four women were executed for witchcraft. Two of them, Rebecca West and Rose Holybred, protested their innocence but Margaret Lundis and Susan Cook confessed to flying through the air, and a whole series of devilish deeds. Three years later Mary Ellis suffered the same fate. Witches were usually hanged but near Little Shelsey is a hollow known as Witchery Hole and tradition has it that witches were burned there. When a strong wind blows from the north the locals say that the wind comes from Witchery Hole.

A whole series of charms were thought to protect you from a witch's curse. Worcestershire was famous for the whitty pear, a small, black, bitter pear which served as a protection against evil. The mountain ash, or Rowan, protected you against evil and sprigs were nailed over doors. Lola Taplin, licensee of the Fleece in Bretforton for many years until 1977, painted white lines over the cracks in the floor to keep out the witches.

The White Witch of Kidderminster

By the middle of the eighteenth century, persecution had died out and witches were able to ply their trade once more. Becky Swann, sometimes known as Betty Swann, lived in either Comberton Hill or Worcester Street (or both) and her death was recorded in 1850. Her healing powers and her ability to find lost property were well-known for miles round. One of her charms for ill-health was the Toad Bag. For this, a live toad had its legs broken and was then sewn into a bag and hung around the patient's neck.

She was prosecuted for obtaining money by false pretences and prophesied that the magistrate who convicted her would not live to see her released from prison. He died unexpectedly soon afterwards, which enhanced Becky's reputation considerably.

Becky is said to have died in a manner befitting a witch. One day, an enormous black cat appeared in the village and clawed at Becky's front door. Becky turned pale when she saw it and let it into the house. Nothing was seen of Becky or the cat for three days, no smoke came from the chimney and the door was locked and bolted. Neighbours broke down the door on the fourth day, the cat fled howling up the chimney and all that remained of Becky was a pile of ashes on the floor.

Kidderminster's Ghost Walks

Here is one of Alan Lauder's tales, manager of Kidderminster Ghost Walks (telephone number: 01562 630046).

In an area near the canal just off New Road in Kidderminster there was once a cornmill known as Caldwell mill. The mill stood in the grounds of the Caldwell Estate, originally owned by the Clare family from approximately 1230. Later the estate was passed to the Earl of Dudley and became the seat of that family.

The miller's name was Francis Best. Every Saturday morning at 9.30 Francis, being a man of habit would take, as he described, 'A most pleasant stroll on a public footpath over Spring Grove', which is where the West Midlands Safari park now stands, to Bewdley market.

On 8th June 1771, he was set upon, a struggle ensued and Francis was stabbed. His assailant was John Child, a journeyman weaver from Wribbenhall. Often described as idle and ne'er-do-well, he was easily recognised by his club foot. Realising that he had been seen, he swiftly rifled the not yet cold body, taking the princely sum of twelve sovereigns, and fled the scene. The body was recovered, and when checked over it was discovered that the killer had overlooked in the waistcoat

Town Hall and Vicar Street, Kidderminster.

pocket the sum of sixty-five sovereigns. Sometime later Child returned to hire a horse to make good an escape to the small town of Birmingham. Before he could set out, he was recognised and apprehended.

The following day, Child denied the crime, naming another as the perpetrator, but admitted being an accomplice. By the Monday, Child had made an attempt to take his own life, with a kitchen knife. He was taken for trial at Worcester, where he was found guilty, and ordered to be hanged on the 18th July 1771, with his body to be taken for dissection.

For a period of time Child was held in heavy shackles at Spring Grove Mansion, and in the words of a man who has connections with this property, 'I will not enter the mansion unattended either during the day or early evening, or at all late at night. I have heard the sounds of a shackled and injured foot being dragged across the floor in the upper storeys of the house'.

Spring Grove Mansion is the large house in Bewdley Safari Park built by Samuel Skey, an ordinary, working-class young man, who was apprenticed in Bewdley to a grocer. When he was sent on errands to Kidderminster he fell in love with the area now occupied by the Safari Park and vowed to build a house on Jackeystone Hill. He unexpectedly inherited £1,000 and started a grocery and drysaltery business in Bewdley. He became rich enough to build a grand house on top of the hill and also to buy up the land around it.

On one of these ghost walks, a teenager by the name of Tracey announced that a ghostly shadow had been seen at her house. Her family were contacted and the following story emerged:

A friend of ours who lives up the road came here one evening and as he was sitting by the living room door he went all cold and felt something walk past him. He went deathly white.

Apparently, that's not the first time something has been seen here. The man next door tells us that he was walking past the house and he saw a shadow at a window when the house was empty. Another time, a child was seen at a window when we were not at home.

A few strange things happen. Sometimes we are all sitting here and we hear noises as if someone is upstairs. We do have doors slam. My husband was lying awake in bed in the early hours of one morning and he distinctly heard a downstairs door slam. No-one had broken in or anything, there was no reason for it. The only other strange thing is that we have all been sitting here and the video has ejected itself, or sometimes it starts rewinding in the middle of a programme when no-one has touched the controls.

Our dog won't go into one particular bedroom. It's the baby's bedroom and he cries a lot in there. Sometimes we hear him talking to somebody. He's only two-and-a-half and we can't make out what he's saying but he's definitely having a conversation.

The Seven Stars Shines Again

Participants in the Kidderminster ghost walks meet in one of the most haunted pubs in England, Ye Olde Seven Stars, which seems to feature in almost every collection of ghost stories. Once a hostelry of bad repute, it is now a listed building opposite the Swan car park and one of the few authentic olde worlde pubs. Alan Lauder of the Kidderminster Ghost Walks was delighted when a strange incident occurred:

Just after 7 o'clock on Saturday, 25th September, I was in the Seven Stars with my wife and teenage daughter, waiting for the lucky participants of that night's ghost walk to arrive. We were sitting round the small table in the front bar having a drink when we noticed a man looking through the pub window at us. My daughter and I began arguing as to who he was looking at and why. My daughter said he was looking at her because she's pretty and I said that if he was looking at her, it was because he thought she was the grey lady. At the mention of the grey lady, the bell at the bar started ringing very loudly and very fast. The barman came running in, wanting to know who had been ringing the bell. We told him that it wasn't us, it had rung all by itself.

Another incident at the pub came to light from Gary, who was a bartender in the summer of 1989. The landlord asked him if he would mind painting the cellar, together with another young man, Mark, who worked part-time at the pub. At that time not only were barrels and bottles kept in the cellar, but the various machines and the juke box were there also. Gary says:

It was just after lunch in the early afternoon, and we were busy painting away. We felt someone come into the cellar – you know what

The Seven Stars, the most haunted pub in England.

it is, you can see somebody out of the corner of your eye. We didn't
bother to turn round because somebody or other kept coming into the
cellar every now and then to see how we were getting on. We turned
round after a few seconds and there was this silhouette of a woman –
just the silhouette and it seemed to be filled with smoke, but you could
see through it. We couldn't believe it, we looked at it for a few seconds
with our mouths open, then we looked at each other and looked back
at the silhouette again but it had gone.

They ran up the steps to tell the licensee who was immediately on
to the local newspaper. He gave Gary and Mark a fiver each for seeing
the ghost.

The Transcendental Kind

For some unknown reason, painters and decorators seem to be popular with ghosts. There are many instances of men in this profession
having a paranormal visitor. One example comes from Comberton
Hill:

My father was a painter and decorator. He was working with a young lad at a large empty house, way up past Severn Valley Railway Station, when they saw an old lady come down the stairs, turn round and go into one of the rooms. They looked at one another and said, 'Did you see that? Where did she come from?'. They went into the room, nobody was in there and there was no way out. They both saw it. It put the fear of God into them.

Kidderminster (ACE) Radio

Kidderminster now has its very own radio station which is called 107.2 ACE FM, broadcasting to the Wyre Forest Area. At present ACE FM is a trial Radio Station broadcasting twice a year for a month at a time until a full licence is granted by the Radio Authority. It's hugely popular with many avid listeners who love the variety of music and chat. The Radio Station is based on the upper floor of a rambling 1930s building which was partly private accommodation prior to its full commercial use today. It is sited on the busy Worcester Road leading into Kidderminster.

Steve Grant, the Station's Manager and Morning Show Presenter reports:

> We moved into the building early in 1999. Soon after, strange things started happening. Jason, one of our DJ's, saw a set of headphones move across the mixing desk of their own accord. There have been problems with the equipment, on occasions starting up on its own when it shouldn't have done. The atmosphere in Studio 1 is always highly charged with static electricity, and although we have anti-static prevention throughout there has been many a victim of an unwanted jolt, myself included. I was told by an expert in the paranormal that static discharge can be one of the signs of an unwelcome guest from the other side.
>
> Out in the corridor the temperature will drop for no reason. You can feel a definite presence, and on more than one occasion this has spooked me so much the hairs on the back of my neck have stood on end. I asked a local ghost hunter who is also a respected accountant, to investigate further and he is no doubt that the building is haunted. He says there are two entities and he is convinced that one of them is looking for a lost insurance policy.

Sue, one of our telephone girls, saw two shadows disappear through the wall of the Studio, one was short and dishevelled the other tall, thin and wearing a hat.

Vanessa Steel is a medium and has been a guest on my show many times. I took her to explore the back stairwell. She looked up to where the light fitting is and said, 'I don't really like what I see up there'. She refused to tell me what she saw but James, one of the Breakfast Show Presenters, told me that he has seen the apparition of a tall thin man wearing a hat, hanging by the neck from the stairwell, a very frightening experience.

One morning at six o'clock the only people in the station were Debbie, Jason and James. They all heard bangs on one of the doors towards the back of the building, which is completely enclosed. The three of them went out to investigate the noises, no-one was there.

On another occasion, when coming in to present the Breakfast Show, James climbed the back stairs on to the landing and he saw, coming towards him from the corner of the landing, a very dishevelled-looking bloke, a short man who stared directly at him. The vision was flailing its arms around and the face was contorted into a vicious looking grimace, it seemed to want James to move out of the way. The most frightening thing was, the apparition was totally silent, it just seemed to glide along, mouthing words but with no sound at all.

All Hip and Happening

Whenever the personalities from ACE radio have a get-together the conversation usually turns to past experiences of the paranormal. Steve Grant tells the story:

Those of you who have seen my photo will not believe it when I tell you that, in the days of my youth, many years ago, I worked for John Anthony as a trainee hairdresser.

In the new salon upstairs it was very early 70s and all hip and happening. But on the first landing was a row of cubicles like the ones you get in hospitals today, each kitted out with a beehive-style hairdryer, and we had a stylist who looked after the old ladies.

At ten to nine one morning I happened to look into one of the cubicles and saw an old grey lady sitting in the chair. I went to the stylist and said, 'Your first client's in'. She was a bit prim and proper and snapped, 'No, she's not'. I told her that there was somebody sitting in the cubicle. Then I walked down to reception and said, 'You've sent somebody up early'. The receptionist's reply was, 'We haven't, the doors aren't open yet'. I went back up and took a look and, of course, nobody was there.

The Bull Ring Kidderminster.

Floating in Mid-Air

Ken Francis is a professional photographer but frequently he's a DJ on ACE radio:

I have had some strange experiences in my old house, this is going back some years when I was about sixteen. My mother had died about two years previously.

We got used to weird things happening. I would hear footsteps and movements in my bedroom but nobody would be there. One evening, we were watching the telly and the three pin plug jumped completely out of the socket. This happened three times.

I remember going into the bathroom, putting my radio down, and turning round to find it floating in mid-air. I just grabbed it and put it back down.

You would put a pen in front of you, turn round, turn back and it would have disappeared. It would be over the other side of the room. I remember this happened to my father's razor once. He was very annoyed.

My father had a Saint Christopher round his neck and once, when he was in the bathroom, we heard the necklace chink and it had fallen in the bath. Fair enough, perhaps the clasp had broken or the chain, but when we picked it up the clasp was still fastened and every link was intact.

One evening I turned to see a brown blob disappearing out of the passage. The two dogs rushed out and I went to see what the hell was going on. When I got to the kitchen the other side of the hallway nothing was there. The two dogs were sitting looking round and the cat was stretched out comfortably in the chair.

We lived in a terraced house. We hadn't said anything to the girl next door but one night she came rushing round to our house and said that she had seen somebody sitting in her kitchen in Edwardian or Victorian clothes. That's when we told her about all the goings-on in our house.

The Phantom Friend

On the outskirts of Kidderminster is a large family home. A daughter of the family, Clare*, begins the story:

> Thirty years ago, when I was aged between about five and nine, I often used to play with this friend. To be quite honest, I can't remember all that much about it. I don't know how often she came, but I do remember her quite clearly. She wore a long white Victorian dress and I think she had a blue sash with a bow or something. She had long blond hair and she was a bit older than me. We played together, I remember that I had some paper dolls and she and I used to dress them with these paper clothes. She seemed very real to me.

Clare's mother tells her side of the story.

> Normally, when my children went to bed, that was it, but often we caught Clare out on the landing. She would say, 'I'm playing with my little friend'. Children do talk to themselves but she seemed to be talking to someone.

When she was nine she went to boarding school. About two years after she had gone away something very strange occurred. Our house was an old family house with a long dark landing without windows; even in the daytime we had to have the light on but this happened in the evening when it was dark. Various doors and staircases went from this landing and there was an airing cupboard one end and Clare's bedroom the other. One evening, my husband was out with my two boys at choir practice, I was alone in the house and standing at the airing cupboard, sorting it out or something, when I felt as if someone was behind me. I turned round and saw this girl in a white nightdress coming along the landing towards me. My thought was, 'Oh, it's Clare' and I said, 'What are you doing out of bed?'. The child never spoke. I must have turned back to the airing cupboard again because I suddenly thought, 'It can't be, Clare is away'. I looked back again and the child was still there, coming towards me. I can see her in my mind's eye now. She was about the same age as my daughter and she had a heart-shaped face and a sharpish fringe with long blond hair almost to the waist. Her hair was parted in the middle and fell each side of her face as if it had just been brushed. The nightdress was quite full and billowed out as she walked, it had a high neck and long sleeves, there was a frill round the sleeves and round the neck where it was fastened by a band. Her feet were bare. She walked slowly, looking straight ahead, she could have been looking at me or she could have been staring into space. She turned a corner, still looking straight ahead and went up the attic stairs. It never occurred to me to follow her up there and see what was going on. I was just transfixed. I saw her for quite a long time and I never felt that she was menacing or sinister. I thought there must be somebody in the house.

I knew it must have been what my daughter had been seeing. I didn't say anything to anyone, I always felt that if I mentioned it to someone it might break the spell. Several years later when we had left the house we did have a talk about it and my daughter could remember seeing and talking to a little girl. It was just incredible and the memory has never left me.

We moved out about thirteen years ago. We were very happy in that house and the family who live there now are also happy.

The Crystal Maze (Park Gates)

Park Gates is on the A451 Stourbridge Road and although the postal address is Wolverley, it's only just outside Kidderminster. The licensee says that they don't have regular customers, most people in there are passing by and just calling in for food. Steve Carrigan was working there as assistant manager in 1999:

One night, I stayed up late. I had cleared away, tidied up and locked the doors, then I decided I would have a go on a new games machine, Crystal Maze. I probably stayed up until about one o'clock. As I was playing on the machine, out of the corner of my eye I caught sight of a figure with blond hair walk from the front door to the kitchen. I thought I was seeing things but I thought I had better go and have a look. The kitchen door was swinging to and fro. It has one of those double hinges and is very heavy and there's no way that a gust of wind could cause that.

Anyhow, I ignored it and went back to the machine. No sooner had I started the first game when I could smell food cooking, like a steak being fried. I went to the kitchen to check it out and nothing was there. It was all quite bizarre.

My first thought was that somebody had broken in, so I set the alarm. As I did that and closed the door, I quite clearly saw a figure at the top of the stairs, outside the door of the first floor flat. It was about thirty years of age, five feet tall with blond hair and definitely female. You could tell it wasn't a real person because it wasn't that solid. I can't remember what it was wearing and it was slightly hazy so that I couldn't see its features clearly. It began to walk along the corridor.

I rushed up the stairs but nobody was there.

A few strange things have happened at the pub after it was renovated recently. The old cellars were blocked over and new cellars opened at ground level. There are about twenty witnesses to the fact that a full bottle of whisky exploded at the back of the bar. We sent the pieces back to Johny Walker's, the distributors, and they had the cheek to tell us that we must have dropped it because there is no way a full bottle of whisky could explode.

Grey Ladies and Twenty Pinters (Wolverley)

Fred Leeson, a member of the local Historical Society, talks about the ghosts of Wolverley:

I have heard it said many times that a grey lady has been seen in the village, she has visited several pubs and houses.

My sister, Joyce, was coming home late one night some years ago and she saw this old fellow – he crossed the road at High Low Bank. Joyce spoke to him but he never answered, then he suddenly disappeared. We all laughed and said she'd been drinking but it couldn't have been that because she was teetotal.

By the traffic lights at the top of the hill is a house known as 'The Birches'. I was going past the house in the 1940s or 50s when a young girl ran out screaming, 'I have seen her, I have seen her!'. I stopped and asked her who she'd seen. She told me it was Miss Hancox who used to live in the house. I said, 'But Miss Hancox died about ten years ago!'. She said, 'I know, but I've just seen her'. Miss Hancox was the kindest and sweetest of people. I said to this young girl, 'Miss Hancox would never have hurt you when she was alive and she's not going to hurt you when she's dead' but she wouldn't have it. She wouldn't go back in the house.

Miss Hancox was very religious. She heard how the blacksmith could swear and she was determined to get him into chapel. She got him to promise to go, but just before he went, his friends went to his house with a lot of wine. Anyway, he staggered up the road to go to the chapel and when Miss Hancox saw him, she said, 'The Lord God would strike you dead if you stepped into my chapel like that'. So he didn't go.

The most haunted pub in Wolverley was the Live and Let Live. That was a ghostly place, that was. It's still in the village but it was converted into flats some years ago. You can see the lettering for the pub on the gable end, Joules Stone Ales. The taps were sometimes turned on and they could often hear somebody draw the beer. They used to hear footsteps going backwards and forwards overhead. My dad was a plasterer, he was working in there one night after hours, in a little room at the side of the passage, when the Cornish latch flew up and the door slowly swung open. Howard Richards ran the pub and he said it happened nearly every night, somebody was walking

The old rock houses in Wolverley at the end of the nineteenth century.

through. Howard's wife was a Londoner and always wore black. The ghost didn't bother them.

My dad played the piano accordion and one day he took my mother, who was a bit psychic, to the Live and Let Live so that she could wait there for him. When he went to collect her she was standing outside in the alley. He said, 'What's the matter?' and she told him that she tried to go over the back doorstep but she met a cold, invisible wall that wouldn't let her pass.

The Staffordshire and Worcestershire canal runs through Wolverley. It was built in 1772, and at about that time three cottages were constructed in Wolverley next to the lock. Samuel Moulder lived in one of them, he could have been the lock-keeper, but in about 1820 either he or his son began to sell home-brewed beer. These three cottages have now been knocked into one and they're the Lock Inn.

The Lock Inn, Wolverley.

I can remember the Inn fifty years back. The beer came from huge wooden barrels behind the bar and it was sold in jugs about eighteen inches (45 cms) high. There were one or two gangs of men who used to come to the pub every night and whoever 'sat in the chair' had to pay for the jug, then they would pass it round. All the men were fifteen pinters and a couple of them were twenty pinters. When the twenty pinters stood up to go home you wouldn't know that they had touched a drop. One of them weighed 25 stone and when they buried him they had to stop the funeral to widen the grave.

Even in those days the pub had a ghost. We could hear footsteps going up and down one of the walls. One lad who is now in his twenties says that if you offered him £10 to go up the top steps he would refuse. When he was a baby he was taken up those steps and he saw something up there – he never told us what he had seen.

Before James became Assistant Manager of the Lock Inn he was 'a bit sceptical' about hauntings. Now he isn't so sure and says:

We moved here about eighteen months ago. Several people told us that something strange had been going on but I'm a bit sceptical and didn't take any notice. Evidently, the previous tenants had had problems.

After about six months, strange things started happening. Things started moving. Rachel, the manager and I would have a function in the restaurant and we would lay up at night but when we went into the restaurant the next day all the cutlery would have moved and it would be all over the place. I used to live here so I know that the burglar alarms hadn't gone off or anything.

Ever since then objects have tended to go walkabouts. Recently, our chef left her keys in her bag and when she went to get them at the end of her shift, they had disappeared. Everybody was looking for them all evening. They were found at the far end of the restaurant on a table in the window. She hadn't gone into the restaurant at all, there was no need for her to go in there.

A lot of people have heard footsteps upstairs when nobody is there. We had a quiz one night, then afterwards Rachel and her husband and myself were sitting in the lounge when we heard footsteps overhead. We all looked at each other and said, 'Who's that upstairs?'. Rachel's children were away at the time. We looked all over the place but nobody was there.

We have had such interference on the telephone. I can't think how many times we've had someone out to fix it.

The mother of one of our bar staff was helping out by doing some work in the ladies' toilets and she distinctly heard a voice behind her saying, 'Careful'. She turned round but nobody was there. That same day there was a bad accident at the front of the inn. Ladies in the toilets say that they have heard footsteps going up the wall, as if they were going upstairs. In the last six months we have done some structural alterations and discovered that stairs used to go up and across where the toilets are.

One night when I was here on my own, I locked up and went upstairs into my living quarters, then I thought, 'I didn't check the alarm in the restaurant'. I went downstairs and into the restaurant in the dark and this big white cloud came in front of me. I didn't think much of it at the time.

We have had various clairvoyants and psychics coming here for a meal and they have all said the same thing, 'Do you know you have a ghost?' and they have described the same person. They say she is a school-mistress type in a long grey dress, the kind they wore in Victorian times, and she is very happy because she loves children and Rachel has her two children living here. Apparently, the part of the inn she likes best is the restaurant and that's where we have most of the problems. The alarm will go off sometimes during the night for no reason and it has always been activated in the restaurant.

About five years ago the Assistant Manager was bottling up in the cellar when he saw her. He left and never came back. But I find the atmosphere here nice. I'm often here on my own and I never feel afraid.

Is Anybody There? (Harvington)

The stump of an old tree standing in front of Harvington Hall is all that remains of a straight avenue of trees which went from the Hall to Chaddesley Corbett and enabled the occupants to see for some way who was paying them a visit. This was essential for the house was occupied by several Roman Catholic priests and for five years from 1678, these priests were hunted down and executed. One man, Titus Oates, had accused the Catholics of plotting against the King and had whipped the country into anti-Catholic hysteria. Catholic books and relics were publicly burned. Some 30,000 Catholics fled from London. Women carried pistols and houses were barricaded against a suspected Catholic uprising. Two priests who spent many years at Harvington Hall were Father Wall and Father Kemble, both were executed. The house has more priests' hiding holes than any other house in England. Not far from the Hall is an old cottage. The back of the house is fourteenth century and the front is late sixteenth or early seventeenth. The occupier says that all was peaceful until:

In the middle of the 1990s, my wife and I decided to divorce. She continued living in the house for a year and you can guess what the atmosphere was like. We heard all kinds of peculiar noises in the house. It was full of creaks and groans – you get used to the usual noises and these were quite exceptional. Four wooden stairs lead into the front bedroom and I have heard a woman's high-heeled footsteps going up three steps when my wife was fast asleep in bed.

I was in bed in the one bedroom, the dog was asleep in the kitchen and my wife was asleep in one of the front bedrooms. Suddenly, at two or three o'clock in the morning, the three of us were woken up by a mighty rhythmic banging on a door downstairs, bang! bang! bang! bang! It was a really hefty bang. The dog started barking. I jumped out of bed and ran into a front bedroom which overlooks the front of the house. We have a gravel drive and nobody was there and nobody was running away. In any case, I would have heard them crunching on the gravel. We have two oak doors in our front porch and both of these are a thin oak, not the kind to give that heavy bang. Being romantic, it sounded like metal striking a door – a sword hilt or something. I ran out of the house and along the drive and looked up and down the road. Nobody was there and no car was about. I could see into the distance both ways. Round our garden is a hedge and a fence so no-one could have got out without my seeing them.

When my wife and I began talking about this, we decided that the sound hadn't come from the front door, but from a door further along the house. When we did some alterations we had discovered an old door which had been bricked up when the stairs were put in years ago and the noise had been coming from there.

At another time I saw the face of my late ex-brother-in-law looking in through the window. He was very close to his sister, perhaps he had come to see what I was doing to her. Another night I woke up to feel some big bloke getting into my bed. He tried to push me out! I'm not the nervous type but it frightened the life out of me. I was in a cold sweat.

Before this time I was a real sceptic. I would hear about these things and put them down to imagination. Now I often wonder if the undercurrent of tension unleashed some kind of energy.

MALVERN AREA

 alvern Priory, like Evesham Abbey, has its origins in a vision. Each account of the story varies, but piecing them together, the following seems to be the broad outline: Werstan was a monk at Deerhurst and when the Danes destroyed the monastery in about 1016 he fled twelve miles north, through marsh and thicket, to the Malvern Hills. There, in a grove of sycamore and wild cherry trees near to St Anne's well, he lived a solitary and holy life as a hermit. One night St Peter appeared to him in a vision and said that he should tell the King (Edward the Confessor) that he (the King) was released from his vow to make a pilgrimage to Rome. This was to be confirmed by messengers from the Pope arriving that very day. Werstan was also to tell the King that he should establish a Benedictine monastery at Westminster. The hermit wrote an account of his vision, sealed it with wax and took it to the King who had just received the letter from the Pope and was most impressed. Consequently, Westminster Abbey was founded with connections to a little cell at Malvern.

It appears that a neighbouring landowner wanted to remove Werstan and so the hermit appealed to Edward the Confessor who granted him possession of a piece of land on which to build an oratory. However, Werstan was apparently murdered and a man known as Guido, perhaps a Dane, was implicated. Guido and his friend, Aldwin, planned to go on a pilgrimage to Jerusalem but the Bishop of Worcester persuaded them to stay in Malvern, telling Aldwin that 'God will do great things for Malvern'. Aldwin set to work establishing Malvern Priory on the land given by Edward the Confessor which soon acquired thirty monks.

Excerpts from the story are given in the beautiful fifteenth century stained glass windows of Malvern Priory.

The Priory had one great enemy – the local witch. Despite the fervent witch-hunting which lasted right up until the days of George II, witches still existed.

Saint Werstan in the painted window of Malvern Priory.

Shakespeare has three of them in Macbeth, meeting at dead of night and hovering around an evil cauldron. The witch at Malvern was so famous that Daniel Defoe (author of *Robinson Crusoe*) writing in the early 1700s, refers to her.

Malvern's antiquarian and historian, Reverend Symons, was fascinated by Malvern's witch, Mary of Eldersfield and refers to her in several novels. He sets Malvern Chase in the 1400s, when most of the Malverns were covered by vast forests and describes the witch's lair as follows:

> There were no trees, but the entire area was covered with dense impenetrable scrub of gorse, honesty, ivy and brambles. Here was a strange structure of wooden logs, interlaced with twigs and bedaubed with mud. It was circular, with four slits looking north south east and west, down narrow paths cut in the scrub ... Inviting us to enter, our guide drew a bench from under a table and motioned us to be seated. Two brown owls, known as 'hooters' blinked upon us from a wicker cage and large raven hopped upon the floor. With these, in apparent intimacy, was a large black cat, and outside in a box of wooden strips, a blackbird was singing with all his might. A small wooden bedstead, a bench, a table, and a wooden cupboard was all the furniture the hut contained. On the table was a parchment covered with groups of stars, and a number of dried plants arranged in bundles; also several adders were dried and hung by their tails from the wooden logs of the walls. Dried newts hung about in clusters.

Later in the story, the witch's hideout was discovered:

> Several men-at-arms appeared leading, or rather dragging, Mary of Eldersfield, with the cry too often heard, 'The witch! The witch!'.

The monks of Malvern Priory were ordered to meet in the chapter house to arrange 'to search into the witchcrafts, sorcery, and dealings with the devil in the neighbourhood'.

> 'evidence had been found ...sufficient to convict a score of witches, for that the place was full of devilish and unholy charms. There were adder skins, the power of which would give the palsy and infernal beetles which would make the cows udder discharge the milk of their own accord; and there was a broomstick which enabled the

sorceress to go to the moon and to milk the lunar cow, thus obtaining lunar butter, which would heal incurable wounds, and consequently persuade those who knew no better that the wicked sorceress was no witch but a wise woman, and so lead them on to their own destruction.'

Reverend Symonds was convinced that the witch of Eldersfield was nothing more than a talented herbalist, with an expert knowledge of remedies for a wide range of afflictions. His theory was that the Witch of Eldersfield was the daughter of Roger Bolingbroke, acquaintance of Henry VI, who was executed at Smithfield for necromancy against the young King.

One of a witch's basic skills is said to be that of fortune-telling. Gillian was amazed by the accuracy of her fortune-teller's predictions:

Twenty-five years ago I went to see a fortune-teller in Malvern. He was marvellous. He said that I would remarry – at that time I was happily married to my first husband and so the thought of remarriage appalled me. I told him it was nonsense, but I did remarry. He said that it would be someone in uniform. Well, he's on the stage so I suppose that counts.

The fortune-teller said that I would have two grandchildren. I thought that was impossible as my daughter had been told that she could never have children. However, she went to see an infertility specialist and she now has two children. He said that one would be very bright and the other artistic and that has proved to be correct. He also said that I would have a successful career and eventually run a business of my own. All that has come about.

Are You Being Served? (Great Malvern)

Just as you were leaving Great Malvern on the Ledbury road (the A449) there was once a large department store, Warwick House, on the left hand side. This was originally a high-class Victorian store, where the shoppers rolled up in carriages and where goods were delivered by the staff. It tried to modernise and even opened a delicatessen department but it couldn't survive and closed down in about 1992. Their maintenance engineer, Frank, says:

I started there in about 1977. They had a ghost there – it was a lady. She seemed to be particularly interested in newcomers. Sometimes, a new girl would be down in the lower area where the kitchens and the tea bar were and this Victorian lady would appear and disappear. They usually grabbed their coats and never came back. It was difficult to get a description of her because a lot of the girls who saw her left straight away. From what I understand, she was wearing dark clothing and they usually described it as Edwardian, which I assume meant a long skirt and puffed sleeves. She was of a late middle-age. Occasionally, the every-day staff would see her too. One girl was particularly prone to this sort of thing and saw her several times.

Warwick House, just before conversion into flats.

I used to be working all hours and would often be in the store at 9 o'clock at night when everybody had gone home. I never saw her although I felt her presence. There was one particular area at the top of the building where I used to feel that someone was watching me and I would turn round and be surprised to find that nobody was there. In the end I ignored the feeling, it didn't bother me. A lot of people felt a presence there.

I had a workshop down in the basement and I used to make certain that I closed all the cupboards before I left at night because of the tools and other equipment, but when I went back in the morning the cupboards would be open. This only happened for the first few months I was there.

We had an Alterations Room. I was working in there one day and taking down some very old fittings when there was a smell of lavender perfume. It was very strong, almost as if someone was standing there, watching. It was an old-fashioned perfume, very heavy. The girls had smelt it before, it used to come and go.

At the end of the ladies' underwear department were several fitting rooms where the lingerie was hanging on metal hangers on a chrome base. As you moved the hangers along you would hear this scraping noise. Several of the girls heard this noise and went into the fitting rooms to investigate. The hangers had been moved along but no-one was there.

We got to like her in a way. Apart from one or two loud crashes she was never any trouble. We asked around to see if anyone had any idea who she was. Nobody could remember anything terrible happening there like an accident or a murder. The only thing they could think of was that back in Victorian times some of the staff used to live in, there were six or seven little rooms for them up in the Gods. We thought it might be one of the old staff who was reluctant to leave.

Just before the place closed down one or two strange things happened. In the same department where I had felt her presence (ladies' underwear and nightdresses) were two large fitting rooms. At nine o'-clock one night there was an almighty crash. I rushed upstairs, thinking that the ceiling had fallen down or something, but not a thing was out of place.

Since the store closed there have been no more reports of the ghost. She was certainly very sociable and perhaps she decided to leave when the place was empty.

Warwick House is now being converted into flats.

Restoring the Spirit of a House

John does restoration work, mostly to churches but he occasionally restores houses.

I have some stories to tell! In Strensham church in the early 1960s I discovered some fine early wall paintings. There was only one discovery which gave me nightmares and that was at Quatt. We discovered a warrior in a crude square box grave. He was covered in leaves and he had a big buckle on his belt. It was so unusual it haunted me for some time afterwards.

Every property has its aura but one house really gave me a weird feeling and that was in West Malvern. It was a beautiful, very early

Victorian house of Malvern stone with seven or eight bedrooms. I worked there from 1957 to 1968. When I started working on it, it was derelict and looked just like a haunted house.

I had a young chap working with me who had come straight from school. An old housekeeper told us about the ghost but we both laughed. Then when I went on to the top landing, I could feel a presence. The longer you were in the house the worse the feeling became, the presence seemed to get more and more disturbed. I can't explain the exact feeling and some people will say, 'You are crackers' but one or two strange things happened. We were sitting there at about two o'clock one day when the central heating tap blew out of one end of the radiator. There was no reason for it. On another day, we were sitting up there, eating our lunch when this young chap said, 'Cor, I've just felt somebody brush past me'. He wouldn't stay up there. We found out later that a man had hung himself there.

I still see the young chap who is now forty and every time I see him we talk about it.

The Surprise Visitor

The following story is for those who believe that, when ghosts appear to the bereaved, it is because of wishful thinking on the part of the bereaved. The narrator lives alone in a large Victorian house in Malvern.

The story which I'm going to tell you happened about two months ago. I lost my wife towards the end of the year 2000, and since then a couple of ladies have come from an agency once a week to do the essential cleaning.

About two months ago two ladies arrived. The one was elderly, she had been several times and she was with a young girl aged about eighteen or twenty that I hadn't seen before. She looked like the older woman, it may have been her daughter.

I took them down to the servants' quarters by the kitchen, they usually started there with the vacuuming. There was a room in the old servants quarters which had not been used for some time and I told them they could clean it. While they are here I usually shut myself in the study which is just off the hall to get a bit of peace and quiet. On this particular occasion I had only been in my study for ten minutes

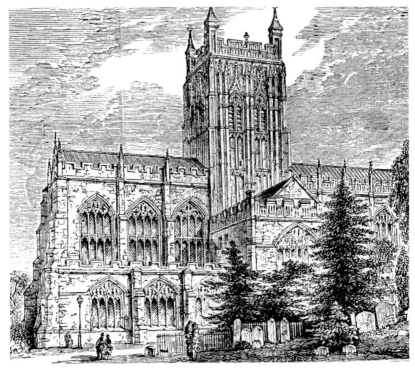

Malvern Priory at the end of the 19th century.

when the elderly lady knocked on the door. She said, 'I see that you have a guest'. I thought she was being mildly facetious and said, 'Do you mean a stray cat or something?' but the woman replied, 'I wanted to ask you if she is staying. Shall I arrange a room for her?'.

I replied, 'What are you talking about? I haven't got a guest'. She said, 'Well, the young girl went down to the room in the servants quarters, she opened the door and saw a lady there'. She didn't say anything but came up to ask the older woman what to do. She went down the stairs, knocked on the door and when there was no reply, looked inside. The lady appeared to have gone. I remarked, 'She can't have gone. Even if she had been there, how could she have got out? The front door is shut and there is a draft excluder on it which makes a scraping noise when it's opened. And I would have seen someone on the drive'. All this time I was looking at them to see if they were playing some kind of joke but they didn't seem to be amusing themselves, in fact they looked quite circumspect.

They were there for about an hour and as they left I asked the young girl, 'Can you tell me any more about this lady?'. She told me that she was wearing a pink rose-coloured cardigan and had brownish hair coming down to her shoulders. My wife did have a rose-coloured cardigan but this was hardly my wife as her hair had gone grey, however, she did have brown hair down to her shoulders when she was young. Then this was the bit that got me. The young girl said, 'There's a photograph upstairs with her on it and you are on it too'. It was my wife. They left and I haven't seen them since.

It never happened again, not to me or to anyone else. Every week the agency sends me cleaners and I ask what happened to those two ladies but there's always some excuse, the elderly lady was ill or her husband was ill, or she's working somewhere else. I wonder if the young lady was frightened but she didn't seem to be afraid at the time, just as amazed as I was.

Why did she appear to them and not to me?

The Shadow of Raggedstone Hill

According to an old legend, there was once a monk from Little Malvern Priory who behaved so badly that, for a punishment, he was told to crawl up the Raggedstone Hill on his hands and knees every day for a year. Eventually he died, and with his dying breath he cursed everyone upon whom the shadow of Raggedstone Hill should fall. The occupier of this cottage has a strange visitor but, sadly, she doesn't think that it's a monk:

This cottage is built in the Georgian style, at the foot of Raggedstone Hill and opposite a bridlepath. Just after we moved to live here (in about 1990) I saw someone going past the window to our front door. It's a bay window and I could only just see the top of his head, he had quite long grey hair. I went to the door but nobody was there. I thought, 'Surely, he hasn't gone through the gate and into the garden round the back?' so I went to the back but he wasn't there either. I thought I was imagining things and thought nothing of it.

Later, my husband was standing in the room and he swore someone had gone past the window. No-one was there so I told him what had happened to me. He said that he expected that it was a figment of our imagination.

My younger son was sitting at the table in front of the window and he suddenly said, 'Who is that who has just gone past the window?' That meant that three of us had seen this figure. I happened to mention this to some friends and they told me the tale about the monk who climbed up the hill on his hands and knees. It didn't look like a monk because his hair was quite long and I always thought monks had their hair shorn.

Several times since then I have seen this figure. Just a few days ago I could have sworn I saw somebody.

My Lodger – the Monk (Leigh Sinton)

One mile north from the furthermost northern tip of the Malvern Hills is the tiny rural village of Leigh Sinton.

This corner of Worcestershire, comprising Leigh, Leigh Sinton and Bransford, is steeped in history. At Leigh is the 900-year old church, together with the largest cruck building in the world and Leigh Court, where Old Coles is reputed to ride as swift as the wind in a coach drawn by four horses, with fire flying out of their nostrils.

A lady recently moved into a house in the area:

Leigh Court at the turn of the century. Courtesy Phillip Coventry.

I had not been living in this house for very long when I discovered that I was sharing it with a monk. I came home from work one lunch time, put the kettle on and sat down in the lounge. Immediately, I knew that there was someone in the house with me. I thought it was a burglar. I sat there, straining my hearing and I sensed that he was in the hall.

I didn't walk straight from the lounge into the hall in case I disturbed him, instead I took the dog and crept to the other end of the lounge and looked into the hall from the far end. There, standing in the hall, I could see what looked like a monk. He was quite short and not very old, middle-aged I would say. He was all in white and I thought, 'Why aren't you wearing brown?'. He seemed to me to have a beard, although I thought monks were clean-shaven, and he had wrinkles on his brow. He looked very real. I felt that he was telling me that he was a friar, not a monk.

I thought I had gone mad. You don't expect to meet a monk in your hall at that time of day. The dog was looking at him too, so I knew that he was there. The dog didn't seem at all concerned, he just stood there, watching him. The monk pointed to the wall of my hall and there, where he pointed, was a most beautiful crucifix. I looked at it and thought, 'Where did that come from?'. Then I looked back at the monk but he had vanished. I looked at the wall and the crucifix had disappeared, too.

I rushed round to my friend's to get her help. I was in such a state when I got there. I said, 'Where can I buy a crucifix?'. My friend was looking in the phone book and saying, 'What will it be under?' and I was saying, 'I don't know'. In the end my friend phoned the SPCK bookshop in Worcester and they gave her the address of a Catholic shop so we were able to rush round there. I bought one and put it on the wall.

Another friend came to visit a few days later and when she came she said, 'There's something in the hall'. Later that week, I went to a meeting and someone there said to me, right out of the blue, 'I saw a monk walk in through that door with you'.

I have heard that there was once a Friary at Leigh Sinton.

We have been unable to trace a Friary but there has been a great deal of ecclesiastical activity in the area. The manor of Leigh was held by the Abbots of Pershore until Henry VIII's time, three miles south of Leigh Sinton is Malvern Priory and a mile to the north is Bransford, birthplace of Wulstan de Bransford, Bishop of Worcester from 1338 to 1349.

The Carmelite friars wore a mantle of white wool and were known as Whitefriars.

The Right Way (Storridge)

About a mile and a half west of Leigh Sinton is Old Storridge Common. Perhaps the Rambler's Association should invest in the services of a psychic:

> I was at my friend's house in Storridge and we were eating in the kitchen. From the kitchen you could look out into the garden where a little stream ran three-quarters of the way round. Suddenly, I saw a signpost on the other side of the stream pointing into her garden. It was very old, and I couldn't make out what it said. I looked away and looked back and it had gone. I told my friend and she said, 'The Ramblers Association have been trying to make out that there is a right of way through our garden. They said they have been using it for hundred of years. There's a dispute over it.' I said, 'Well, they must be right because I've just seen the old signpost!'

REDDITCH AREA

n early medieval times, Redditch was a great religious centre. The town grew up around Bordesley Abbey, one of the largest Cistercian monasteries in the Midlands. By 1332 it had 33 monks. After the Black Death of the fourteenth century there were not enough monks to keep the abbey in good repair and by the middle of the sixteenth century the life of the abbey had more or less petered out. When Henry VIII set to work closing monasteries there was very little left at Redditch to dissolve. Over the years the stonework was carried away and used as building material elsewhere, leaving only a little chapel for use of the local inhabitants.

With the arrival of the making of needles, fish hooks and allied trades in the eighteenth century, Redditch prospered. Needles have always been a valuable trading commodity. They were essential items, easily transported. Vast areas of Canada and North America changed hands from the Red Indians to the settlers for a dozen or so packets of Redditch needles. In the Sudan in the mid 1800s a packet of needles could buy you a wife!

The little town prospered and moved uphill half a mile away from the abbey. Consequently, what had once been an abbey town now had no church at all. In 1807, it was decided to dismantle the chapel at Bordesley and use the materials to build a new church in the centre of the little town. It had a clock face for each of the cardinal points and could seat a thousand. John Noake described the new church as an:

> architectural abortion which I have dignified by the name of chapel. Over the western part of the roof is a cupula or miniature dome covered with some dark metal which gives it an appearance of a railway engine boiler.

White Witches in Needle Town

The church was rebuilt in 1845 and still stands at the heart of the town. Although the church was packed every Sunday with an attentive crowd, Redditch folk seemed to have also put their faith in white witches.

Molly Baker used a pack of cards to entertain young girls by forecasting future events. Redditch is unusual in that two other white witches were both male. John Smith's speciality was discovering lost or stolen property. We have a description of him from the William Avery Memorial Volumes as an elderly man, about five feet two or three inches with broad shoulders and a short neck, dressed in a well-worn black coat and a tall black hat. The tails of his coat reached nearly to his heels and the brim of his hat seemed to rest upon his shoulders. He was a man of very few words. Unfortunately, he was too fond of 'tippling' and had to sell his astrological journals, so that whenever he wanted some information, he had to go to a friend's to look at them.

In 1845 he was consulted over missing rabbits, when a young schoolboy found that breeding rabbits was a lucrative hobby:

> With pence saved from time to time he purchased his first pair, and these multiplied exceedingly, as rabbits will, until he became master of a stock that was the envy and admiration of his associates… There came a voice of lamentation in the cottage on the Common, for on rising in the morning to feed his rabbits the boy found the hutches empty and the foundation of his future fortune cut away from under him.
>
> *James Woodward*

The boy's mother went to see John Smith, who told her that the rabbits had been stolen by a friend about five miles away who had visited her son the previous week. This was confirmed when a travelling draper arrived at the door with a quantity of rabbit skins, the colour of which corresponded to the missing pets. He had purchased them from the son's friend.

Then there was Jon Johnson, who sold ointments and medicines for both the inhabitants and their animals, and was known as Dr Johnson. He was consulted by a farmer who wished to know who had bewitched his cows. The doctor told the farmer to cut off some hairs from the cows' tails and burn them at midnight, and then lay his horsewhip on the back of the next person who came into the house so as 'to draw blood upon him' and the cows would give milk again. The farmer followed the doctor's advice and the first unlucky person who to come into the house happened to be 'Old Rodney' from Headless Cross. Poor old Rodney caught a whipping and the cows recovered.

By 1964 the population had risen to 29,000 and Redditch was designated as a new town. The Redditch Development Corporation arrived.

The Kingfisher Shopping Centre.

Unfortunately, it was necessary to demolish the Congregational Church in Evesham Street in order to build the new shopping centre. The fact that part of the centre was built on holy ground has often been blamed for the surprising number of paranormal incidents when the centre first opened. Lifts whizzed up and down in the middle of the night, dark monks glided through doors and along balconies and several times police were called out to the sound of a child crying.

We're Not Alone

Once the centre was established, most of the incidents died out. Every shopping centre has one or two premises which sport a ghost, and Redditch is no exception as one of the sales assistants explains:

I've worked here for six or seven years and there's been something here all that time. The very first day I sensed that someone was here, and on the second day I said to another girl, 'We're not alone, are we?'. She said, 'I'm glad you said that, I've had the same feeling'. Our area manager doesn't like the atmosphere in here. He just pops his head round the door, asks if everything is alright and goes. We don't mind that at all!

When we arrive in the morning there's a knocking going all along the wall, as if someone is saying, 'Watch out, the humans are coming!'. Sometimes we can hear rustling in the store room out the back. One morning one of the shop assistants heard so much rustling that she assumed that the other assistant was out the back. She was amazed when the girl came through a door at the other end of the shop. Sometimes there's a cold whoosh which goes through the place when there's no reason for it.

Our ghost likes to make his presence felt. We put everything nice and tidy, turn round a few minutes later and the corners of everything have been flipped over as if he has been looking through them. We fix a label on a shelf, then a minute later we find that the label has whizzed along to another section. Pens suddenly disappear. Sometimes, we're working with a calculator, we put it down and the next thing we know is that it's over the other side of the shop. We never see anything actually moving, we just find it in another place.

One of the Security Guards was worried one evening after we had closed because the shop appeared to be full of smoke, although he couldn't smell burning. Fortunately a cleaner was nearby who knew we were having problems in the shop. She told him not to worry.

We all have the feeling that somebody is there. I can feel him on the bend in the stairs, then he often stands in the far corner. We all know when he is about because we can smell cigarette smoke – the old coarse kind. Sometimes I can see a dark shape standing there with a hood over his face like a monk. If he's there for longer than a few seconds I tell him to go away and he goes. We tend to get him a lot at Christmas when he seems very sad. The atmosphere seems to get very heavy.

I'm not the only one to see something here. Until recently, we had a door in the back of the shop with a window in it. One of our customers happened to look through the window and she said to us, 'There's a little girl in there'. We went to have a look but nobody was there.

Last Tuesday a little boy came into the shop and while we were serving his mother he poked his head round our storeroom door. He said, 'Why is that little boy in there eating a sandwich?'. Thinking that someone had wandered in, we rushed to have a look but the storeroom was empty.

Until the beginning of 2001, three ladies worked in a large office off Royal Square. One of them says:

> There's a fire exit going up the back and we can often hear someone going up there and when we look out no-one is about. We can also hear someone in the back office moving about. The supervisor will say, I know somebody is in there, go and have a look, but there's never anybody there.

Thornfield Properties plc are redeveloping the Centre. Now, in the summer of 2001 Royal Square is a mass of rubble. Perhaps the Royal Square ghost looks on in bewilderment.

The Extinct Unicorn

Unicorn Hill was named after the Unicorn Inn, the principal inn of the town in the early 1800s. John Noake, who visited the inn at the time, remarked that the landlord appeared to be a person of considerable taste and added:

> The borders of the bowling green are laid out in an agreeable style and adorned with a fine selection of shrubs and flowers. In the interior of the inn I found the walls covered with many superior paintings.

Unfortunately, the Unicorn was not able to maintain its high standard and, despite rebuilding, had such a bad reputation that its licence was withdrawn in 1998 and the building was demolished. All that remains now is the Unicorn motif on a side wall. In *Unquiet Spirits of Worcestershire* young Marcus describes his experiences which led him to believe that the place was haunted. One of Redditch's Social Workers supports his conviction:

> In the early 1980s my children were small and I was glad to find a couple of hours work here and there, so I got a job as a cleaner in the Unicorn Public House, Unicorn Hill, Redditch. I had not been there very long when we had a bad fall of snow. The manager asked me to clean the step with hot water and salt, and afterwards when I had dried the step, to resume my indoor cleaning chores. I was to bolt the door to make sure that no hopeful customers came into the pub before opening time.

The Unicorn when Jessie Castrey was licensee, somewhere between 1850 and 1864. Courtesy Phillip Coventry.

The door was a big wooden old-fashioned door, arching upwards to a height of about ten feet, so to open and rebolt it, one had to hammer the bolt across using the head of a broom. This I did, and after I had bolted the door, I took the broom back to the cupboard, finished my indoor duties and finally went home.

The next day the manager took me to one side and quietly told me that I had not bolted the door the day before, as he had found a couple of customers wandering about in the pub a few minutes before opening time. As the front step had iced up overnight, he wanted me to clear the front step again but this time to make sure that the door bolt was secure! I was mystified at this because I distinctly remembered hammering the bolt home with the broom, but I assumed that the bolt was not fully in place, so I apologised and said I would make sure that the door was secure this time.

I cleared the ice, and dried off the step, gathered my bucket and mop and went back inside. I picked up a big broom and hammered the bolt home, testing the door after me. Satisfied that it was now fastened securely, I took the big broom and the mop back to the cleaners' cupboard, and took out the polishes and Brasso to clean the upstairs lounge. There were two banisters going up the stairs, so I cleaned one going up and turned around to clean the other coming down. As I descended towards the front door, I was amazed to see a man and woman walking towards me. They asked me if the pub was open yet. They must have thought I was mad because I just gaped at them, and finally managed to ask how they got in! They said through the front door. I told them that they would have to go because the pub did not open for half an hour, and saw them out.

I was puzzling over this as I made my way back to the cupboard to get the broom again to bolt the door, when I met one of the other cleaners coming towards me. She could see I was worried about something, so I joked with her that either I was going mad or the place was haunted. The cleaner said: 'Yes, it is haunted. Things go missing all the time, and turn up later in the wrong place, or the vacuum plug gets pulled out so one has to retrace one's steps just to put the plug back. Childish pranks really, nothing to be worried about'.

Apparently, the ghost had been seen in the 'snug' sitting in a corner seat, but only when the lights were off. When the lights were switched on, the ghost disappeared.

I never saw the presence, but I left soon afterwards for another job.

Sun Gods and Blue Suits

Bates Hill, a branch of Unicorn Hill, has suffered in the town's redevelopment. Once a busy through road, it has now been converted into a cul-de-sac. To the south is the rear of the Danilo cinema and on the northern side is the back of the doctor's surgeries and the Apollo Warehouse.

In 1843 a large red-bricked Wesleyan chapel was built on a raised area towering over Bates Hill. This disappeared in the new town development and the Apollo Warehouse was built on this once-sacred site in 1984. David Stanley remembers that thirty years ago he attended his cousin's wedding in the Chapel, then from 1993 until 1999 he worked as an Assistant Branch Manager on the same site. He says:

> The Apollo is on two floors. The shop is on the ground floor and above it is the warehouse. One afternoon I walked up the stairs and went into the warehouse. As I turned to the left I saw somebody walk round the back of some boxed gas fires. He was tallish, of medium build and aged about forty or fifty, with greyish hair. He was wearing a blue suit and I assumed he was one of the warehouse men. I shouted 'Hello!' to him but he didn't reply. I shouted again but he still didn't reply. I walked up to where I had seen this person and nobody was there. I decided it was very strange but I never thought anything of it.
>
> This happened three or four years ago but since then another member of staff has seen the same thing.

The Apollo Warehouse, scene of a blue-suited ghost.

David Perry joined the company in February 1977 as Warehouse Supervisor. One day he was just tidying the warehouse before he went off to lunch, sweeping up a few bits and pieces from the floor, when:

> Nobody had warned me about the ghost. The first thing I knew about it was that I happened to look down the warehouse and I saw

the image of our gas fitter. I saw his face quite clearly. He is in his mid-fifties and wears the official uniform of a blue rollneck shirt and blue trousers. I thought, 'Fair enough' and carried on working. Then I suddenly remembered the gas fitter was on holiday that week. I turned round again and was just in time to see him move sideways at a phenomenal speed and disappear by the back entrance of the gas showroom. I went to have a look but he had vanished.

A bit later I happened to mention it and they told me that David Stanley had seen the same thing a couple of years back. I thought they were pulling my leg. I asked David what he had seen and as he was telling me I was saying the same. We had both seen identical ghosts. I thought, 'This is too spooky for me'.

For a couple of days afterwards I felt an icy patch there. One of the lads came upstairs and said, 'Isn't it cold up here?' and he was standing just where I had seen the ghost.

I thought, 'What have I seen?'. I wondered if something had happened to the gas fitter. I was so relieved when he came back from holiday the next day and he was alright.

A Key Problem

During the 1970s Ann was working in the large offices of the Midlands Electricity Board in Windsor Road:

I had a huge bunch of keys – there was the key to the strong room, the safe key, the petty cash key, the door key and others besides. They were kept in the top right hand drawer of my desk which was always locked. One day, I went to get the keys out of the drawer and they had disappeared! Everyone in the office hunted high and low for them but we couldn't find them. Eventually I said to everybody, 'Stop looking, I'll just have to report them as lost'. The next morning I opened the drawer and there they were. I was the only one with a key to my drawer and it had been locked overnight.

The Post Room and Filing Room was a large office. When my friend was working in there she saw a stranger sitting at one of the desks. She looked again and he had disappeared. He was seen by two different people and one colleague flatly refused to go in there if she would be on her own.

The MEB offices have since been redivided.

Fred and the Young 'Uns

Also in the centre of Redditch, in Ipsley Street, is the Youth and Community Centre. Anne started her work as a caretaker/cleaner in charge in the early 1980s and remained there for many years.

It was more of a Sports Centre in those days, for example, groups used to book a lunch-time session for football, basketball, trampolining or a rock-climbing session. Occasionally individuals wanted to use the multi-gym, and the equipment was stored upstairs. It was my responsibility to open the building in the mornings, and lock up after everyone had left in the afternoons. I also 'let' the rooms, supervised the cleaning and was responsible for any repairs. The full staff complement at that time was the manager; a part-time typist who came in on Fridays; a cleaner and myself.

I had not been there many days when I became aware of the footsteps. They usually happened on the first floor. I thought at first, that children had climbed onto the roof and got in through an open window to play with the multi-gym equipment.

I ran up the stairs ready to tell the children to clear off, but found all the windows firmly shut and the doors closed. This became a regular occurrence and I learned to ignore the footsteps, but occasionally the sound of things crashing to the floor or doors slamming shut had me running up the stairs to find all the doors and windows locked and the rooms as I had left them. The other cleaner and I called our unseen presence 'Fred'. I had the impression that Fred was an old man who had died in a house that had been demolished to make way for the Youth Centre.

Through the years, there were other incidents where things went missing and turned up in other places. I had mentioned the incidents to the manager at first, but he was so obviously a sceptic that I never mentioned them again, even though he was aware of the footsteps.

The only time that I felt uncomfortable with Fred was about a year after I started working there. A group had finished a game, showered and left. I went into the changing rooms to mop up the water, check for lost property and lock up. I had an oppressive feeling and an overpowering urge to GET OUT! So intense was the feeling that I panicked and ran out in a cold sweat. I calmed down and a few minutes later, I steeled myself to go back into the changing room. I felt rather foolish and tried to tell myself that I had imagined it, but I have never felt that feeling of dread in that intensity before or since.

An Embarrassing Manifestation

Near to the town centre is a smart Victorian hotel which has a very embarrassing manifestation:

My housekeeper, Sue* complained to me that there was this terrible smell, just like somebody's smelly feet. It had strange properties – you could walk into the smell and walk out of it so that you knew what size it was. It didn't stay in the one place, it kept following her around.

When she reported that it had gone into room H, I went to investigate and it hit me. Very occasionally we have had a sewage problem and we have had to get someone out to deal with it but this smell was not like that at all. I went back into the lounge and I felt physically sick. At the time two chaps were staying in the room and I heard the one saying to the other, 'Have you been b..... smoking in that room? It smells awful'. It was very embarrassing.

Later it visited the barman and even our general maintenance man smelt it. It would follow us around.

One of the reasons we thought that it was associated with the paranormal was that we have had a number of odd things happening here over a period of time, especially just before Christmas. Sue often feels that there is someone at the side of or behind her but when she turns round, no-one is there. She pooh-poohed her feelings until recently. She was cleaning outside room H when she suddenly went very cold and said she felt as if something had walked through her. I was working with her at the time and we were both had something in our hands, Sue had a clean towel and I had a clean cloth. Neither the cloth nor the towel had a smell on them but when you smelt our hands, they were terrible.

Things also disappear. Last weekend I bought a new dustpan and brush and I know that I put it on top of a fridge but when I went to get it the next day it had disappeared. I hunted high and low for it, it was a vivid lime green, a colour which could not be overlooked. Eventually it turned up hanging on a hook in the wall right in front of your nose as you walked in through the door. If it had been there before I would have seen it.

Sometimes, the staff feel very drained and cold for no particular reason. Our maintenance man said that while he was doing room H he felt absolutely drained. He hadn't felt like that before.

The previous owner has told us that she woke up one night to see a lady standing over her. The owner's daughter says that she always felt that there was something on the stairs.

You can't have a bad smell wandering round a hotel so I called in some paranormal experts. A small group of people arrived and spent about an hour and a half upstairs. Then they came downstairs, and were sitting at the far end of the lounge when one of the men stood up and said, 'I have to go now, I'm going to work tomorrow'. As he left the room, whatever-it-was seemed to go with him. We all felt the atmosphere lift. A week later I was cooking and I caught a whiff of the smell but after that it disappeared, hopefully permanently.

Don't Tell Your Aunt!

Until well into the twentieth century, the Earl of Plymouth was the chief landowner in Redditch, consequently many of the roads in Redditch are named after his family or their associations. In 1682 the title, Earl of Plymouth was given to Lord Windsor of Hewell Grange. The title died out in 1843 but resurrected in 1855 and awarded to a descendent of the Windsors, the wife of Robert Henry Clive. Her grandson became baron Windsor and Earl of Plymouth. We therefore have Clive Road, Windsor Road, Plymouth Road, and Hewell Road. The address of their main mansion was Oakley Park, Salop, so we have Oakley Road and Salop Road. Other (with a long 'o', as in rota) Archer Windsor gives rise to Archer Road and Other Road.

During the 1970s a couple of ghosts seem to have taken up residence in Other Road:

I used to live in Other Road, which is just off Easemore Road. The house was an old Victorian villa, over a hundred years old and three storeys high.

In the evening, when I was ironing or just watching the TV, I used to feel a presence behind me. I knew it was a lady and that she was watching me. It wasn't an unpleasant feeling, I felt that she was a nice person.

One summer in the 1970s my aunt and uncle came to stay with me for a couple of weeks. He was going to the bathroom on the first floor in the early hours of the evening when he saw the grey shadow of a lady in the corner of the landing. He spoke to her, he said, 'Who are you? What are you doing here?' but she just disappeared. The next morning at breakfast he said to me, 'You have got something in the house, haven't you?' and he told me what he had seen. His comment was, 'Don't tell your aunt!'

Another ghost story comes from the same road in the same period. What a pity they don't want to disclose their numbers. Were they next door neighbours?

In the 1970s our family used to live in Other Road, Redditch. I used to sleep with my sister, who was three years younger than me, top to tail. There were two flights of stairs and our bedroom was on the middle flight.

When I was about eight my sister woke up in the night, crying and calling for our mum, and she said that she could see the face of a devil on her hand. Now, it was a rule in our family that we never disturbed my parents at night. Even when we got up in the morning we had to knock on their bedroom door and wait for them to call, 'Come in' before we entered. I tried to quieten my sister myself and I told her, 'Mum and dad can't hear you!'. But she kept on and I decided to go and

Other Road Redditch.

fetch my parents. I came out of the bedroom, went on to the first landing and there was the apparition of an old man barring my way. He looked just like Old Father Time. He had a long white beard and long white hair, very fine and straggly. He was solid white except for about two feet from the floor, when I could see through him. I remember thinking to myself, 'How is it that I can see through him?'. He was pointing at my bedroom door and although his lips didn't move I knew that he wanted me to go back to bed. He didn't look fierce, he had a kind, gentle face. I said to him, 'I can't go back, my sister's too upset' but he just kept pointing. I thought that if I went back into the bedroom for a few minutes he would have disappeared by the time I came out, so I went back into my room but when I came out he was still there in the same position. Then I thought that if I ran at him, he would have to move aside, so I ran at him but I went right through him. I didn't feel cold or anything.

I went into my parents and told them that my sister had had a nightmare. I said, 'By the way, there's a man on the landing'. My dad ran out, thinking that someone had broken in, but no-one was there. He said I was dreaming but I know that I was awake.

Who Goes There? (West Redditch – Lakeside)

Redditch town is almost cut in two by a huge stretch of green running from the Abbey Stadium, through the Bordesley Abbey meadows, to the Arrow Valley Park. Halfway through this stretch of green is the Arrow Valley Lake, an artificial stretch of water which alleviates the flooding which once occurred throughout the valley but particularly at Beoley. Lakeside is on the western borders of Arrow Lake.

Michael, an engineer, is looking for an explanation to his uncanny experiences:

In about 1986, I was living on the Woodrow and I used to travel up Arthur Street to the Studley Road on my way home from work. I often used to work into the early hours and late one night, about 2.15 am, I had just gone past the junction of Arthur Street with Studley Road when I caught sight of a little girl in my headlights. I saw her very clearly, she was about ten years of age, she had long dark hair and was wearing a grey coat with a dark collar. She was nicely dressed, obviously a middle-class girl, and she was walking a little dog on a lead.

I thought, 'She shouldn't be out at this time of night' and I braked and looked in my mirror, but she wasn't there. I had only travelled a few yards. I turned my head and looked round but she wasn't anywhere to be seen. I had been working hard all night and I assumed I was seeing things. I just dismissed it.

About twelve months ago I saw her again. This time I made a note of the date, October 25th, and I remembered that it was about that time of the year that I saw her before. Thinking about it, she was dressed out of the present time, I would say that her coat belonged to the 1930s, 40s or early 50s.

This has really bugged me. Was there a little girl who had an accident there on October 25th? I have been doing some research in the library and I see that in the 1930s there are houses on one side of the road only and the other side of the road is just fields. Yet when I saw the little girl, she was on the field side and she had a wall behind her, but there is no wall there now. The road at that point has a house missing, the numbers are 87, 89, 91, 93 and 97, number 95 is a vacant plot. Was a house there once and did a little girl live there who had an accident?

The Changing Face of Art (Lodge Park)

In the centre of Lodge Park is a natural pool. The western half was a muddy swamp until the Redditch Development arrived, cleaned it up and built a housing development round it.

The appearance of an apparition in paintwork, plasterwork or on a damp wall is a fairly common phenomenon. The anecdotes about the Foxlydiate Hotel include one where the shape of a face repeatedly appears in the plasterwork. A couple who bought an old vicarage scraped the wall down to the brickwork but could not get rid of the outline of a cross. The following story is unusual in that the face changed its expression:

I have a brother who lives in Lodge Park. I helped him to varnish a table and a door. When we finished that night, it did look very good and we were pleased with the finished results.

The next morning, when we inspected our handiwork, we were amazed to see that a face had appeared in the newly vanished door. The face looked like an old man's face, with the hair brushed back

Lodge Pool, Lodge Park.

and a bearded effect. Assuming that we had not rubbed it down properly, I sanded it again and re-varnished it.

The next day the face was back again. I was frightened, and wanted to take the door off, but my brother told me to leave it there. He said that it might bring bad luck to take it off as the 'face' had become angry, so the door is still there. My brother and his wife are quite happy to share their house with the 'face', and it has never bothered them.

The Helpful Ghost (South Redditch)

1999 was a year which Julie* would prefer to forget. Together with her husband and three small children she planned to move to a new house but, although her current house was sold, the one into which she should have moved was accidentally sold to someone else! The family had nowhere to live! For several months they stayed with friends and relatives and were very relieved when a suitable modern semi-detached house became available. Four weeks later the family moved into a new house, believing their troubles were over. Julie takes up the story.

We moved on the Saturday. The following Monday the door upstairs sounded as if it had opened and closed. There is a draft excluder all round the edge and it makes an unmistakable swishing noise. My husband went to check the children but they were all fast asleep. We dismissed the incident as nothing. The next day we heard footsteps coming from the bedroom above us. Again the children were all fast asleep.

I went to work on the Wednesday. When I came home my husband ran a bath for me. I went upstairs to check that everything was ready but came down again at the last minute and noticed that Coronation Street had started. As it's my favourite soap I decided to have a cup of tea and watch the telly for a bit. My husband kept saying, 'Your bath water's going cold' and I told him I could run some hot in. Then we heard dripping noises outside, I looked out of the window to see that the overflow was running. I rushed upstairs to find that the hot tap had been turned full on and it had run for so long that the hot water was running cold.

That same night I was woken up by a whirring noise and went downstairs to discover that the washing machine spin downstairs was going. I also heard footsteps but none of the children were out of bed.

Every morning my husband's alarm goes off at six o'clock. He nods off for a few minutes, then he wakes up and gets out of bed. The following Monday the alarm went off as usual but he went back to sleep so soundly he didn't get up. For no reason at all, the alarm went off again at seven and woke him up. This meant that he was able to get to work on time, had the alarm not gone off he would have been late.

Strange noises come from the bathroom. I have heard the bathroom cabinet opening and closing. I was sitting on the loo when I heard something go ting, ting, ting, tapping all along some chrome shelving on the window sill from one end to the other.

One night I was half asleep when I heard this rhythmic tick, tick, tick. I thought at first it was a clock. We have a large clock in our bedroom and a small travel alarm but it wasn't either of those. It wasn't a regular sound, it would tick a few times then stop, then start again. It seemed to be moving towards the bed. When it had nearly reached the bed it stopped completely.

One Monday morning in the school holidays I was getting ready to go to my friend's and I was running late. I was in my bedroom when I heard a voice on the landing shout, 'Oi!'. I went out of my bedroom to see who it was but nobody was there. My daughter was watching the TV downstairs and she came out of the living room and called up the stairs, 'What did you shout Oi for?'. I assumed this was our ghost saying, 'Hurry yourself up or you'll be late'.

Last week my son woke up feeling unwell. He was in the bathroom being sick when I heard a loud crash from the kitchen. I woke my husband up and asked him to see what the noise was and to get a cloth. He went downstairs and found the kitchen light on. We had definitely switched this off before we went to bed. When I had washed up I had put the plates in the rack then carefully placed the saucepan lids on top of the plates and put an upturned saucepan on top of each lid. One of the lids was on the floor. I don't see how a lid could have fallen without the saucepan moving. The following morning the back door was unlocked. I always lock it, even if I'm just popping something outside.

An old lady lived in this house before us for a long time and she died here. I'm told by the neighbours that she was a really nice, kind, helpful woman. I think she comes back and tries to help us. She ran the hot water into my bath when it was getting cold, she puts the washing machine on, she makes the alarm go off for a second time when my husband had gone back to sleep and she tries to help with the washing up.

She usually pays us a visit about five or six o'clock in the evening when we hear footsteps coming from the bedroom above us, across the landing and down the stairs. The footsteps always come from my bedroom. I'm not the only one who has heard them, my mum has commented on them and so have the kids. There's a cold spot at the end of my bed, we have double glazing and central heating and the house is warm all through except for that spot.

Last Thursday my daughter was on the toilet and she started crying. I asked her what the matter was and she said that she could hear noises coming from our bedroom when she knew we were all downstairs. I told her not to worry and it was only the people next door she could hear. The following night I woke up at about four o'clock and wanted to go to the toilet but I was too afraid. I heard footsteps coming round the bed. I sleep facing my husband and the footsteps came round the back of me to the end of the bed and returned to the door.

Last night I was in the bedroom and I heard a noise coming from the kitchen as if someone were stamping their feet on the floor. My husband heard it too because I saw him looking over the banister to see who it was. A little later, I was sitting in the lounge reading a book when suddenly someone gave a loud tap on the frosted plastic sheeting of the door on my right. The noise is unmistakable as the sheeting is loose and the noise reverberates.

From my own point of view I'm more intrigued than scared but I'm hoping to get something done about it in case it frightens the children. It's already scared my daughter.

Headless Coachmen at Headless Cross

The old road from Redditch to Evesham rises sharply as it leaves the town to arrive at Headless Cross.

By the first half of the nineteenth century it was a wretched, lawless place. Bull-baiting and cock-fighting were popular, together with bare fist boxing:

> The most terrible fighting I ever witnessed was at the White Hart, between a lot of (needle) pointers, who having met there to spend a quiet day, found the time hanging rather heavily on their hands and so, by way of variant, turned out for a fight. They paired themselves according to weight and made the arrangement that no one should be

permitted to fight more than three rounds, but these might be as long as they could make them. Knowing, therefore, how little time they had to 'do business in' you may imagine the manner in which they set to work and execute they did.

William Avery

Saint Luke's church was built in 1867/8, the Victorian villas have now been upgraded and the village has been enhanced by the gift of a hall and a playing field from the general manager of Royal Enfield, as a memorial to his wife.

The name of the village is thought to have no macabre associations and to be merely named after the crossroads where a Mr Hedley lived. However, there is no record of a Mr Hedley and if other villagers have, in the past, seen the same apparition as in the following story, perhaps the name comes from the headless coachman!

Mrs Reynolds says that in 1946 her brother, Donald, was sixteen and a sensible lad, 'as young men were in those days':

He had a motor bike and one evening he and his friend, Tony, decided to go for a run as Donald thought he might have a slow puncture and he wanted to test the tyres. We lived in Wythall and they decided to go for a shandy at a pub in Redditch.

Headless Cross, where a headless coachman has been seen driving a coach and horses. This photograph was taken in about 1910. Courtesy Phillip Coventry.

After the shandy they rode up the hill out of Redditch towards Headless Cross, which in 1946, was very quiet and set in open countryside. It was a long, slow climb so they got off their bikes and pushed them up the last part of the hill. They had almost reached the crossroads when they heard this noise. They said to each other 'What's that noise?' and 'It sounds like horses'. By that time it was dark so they remarked, 'Who would be riding horses at this time of night?'. As the noise seemed to becoming towards them they decided to draw their bikes to one side.

First they saw swivelling lights, then they saw a set of wheels and a coach came rushing past them. It looked quite real except that the driver had no head. The coach swept past, just like that and disappeared. It frightened them so much that they got back on their bikes and came straight home.

They were shaking so much my father and I thought that they had had an accident. I felt quite sorry for them. When my father heard what had happened he started laughing. He said that he had heard many stories about a phantom coach but had never met anyone who had actually seen it.

Donald was so terrified that for the next four weeks he slept with his bedroom light on and he never went anywhere near Headless Cross again.

Don't Look Round Now (Hunt End)

The road through Headless Cross passes Hunt End which marks the southern end of the old Redditch town. One end is firmly in the old Redditch, the other is on the edge of the green belt. Tucked away is a small factory site here where Royal Enfield developed their bicycle factory from Townsend's needle mill. For about ten years Royal Enfield made cars here, as well as bicycles. Afterwards it became a battery factory, then Dunlop's stored tyres there. It burned down in the early 1970s and was converted into a site with small industrial units.

One of the occupiers of a house built on the rural side of Hunt End, has a problem:

Strange things have happened in this house, all in the space of a few weeks, since we gutted the original kitchen and built a new one. I have two daughters, both in their late teens and they each have their own bedroom. One night I heard them both call out, 'Is that you mummy?' thinking that someone had gone up the stairs, but it wasn't me. There's a sweet smell in my bedroom and the smell of cigarette smoke in the house, although we don't smoke.

The younger of the two seems more susceptible to these things. She was in her bedroom one night when she heard whispering. Thinking it was her friend coming out of the bathroom, she called, 'Can you speak up, I can't hear what you're saying'. When she discovered that nobody was there she was quite frightened.

She had a friend to stay over, the friend was sleeping on a mattress on the floor which was next to the bed, so my daughter was on one level and the friend was about three feet below. Her friend woke in the early hours and saw a lady sitting at the end of the bed in this massive glow. She started shaking her feet to make sure that she wasn't dreaming and when she moved her feet, it went.

My older daughter was in her bedroom with her friend when the handle of the bedroom door turned and the door flew open with a bang. There's a thick carpet under the door which makes it stiff to open. We have no idea what made it do that. Nobody was there.

My husband is away a great deal and as I hate being alone, my older daughter sleeps with me when he's away. I don't have a proper night's sleep in his absence and one night I tossed and turned until I dozed off, somewhere between twelve and two in the morning. When I woke up I was on my back with my arms over the quilt, and something seemed to be lying all down the one side to the knee. My face was squashed by something, I tried to turn to look at it but my face was being pushed back, as if to say, 'Don't look round'. I had the feeling that it was a woman and someone that I knew. I wondered if I was dreaming but I was able to move the other arm and leg so I knew that I was awake. When I was able to move my head I looked round and expected to see someone standing by the side of the bed but no-one was there. I thought an animal of some kind might have climbed on to the bed so I sat up and shook the quilt. This woke up my daughter and she said, 'What are you doing that for?' I told her that I was hot so that she wouldn't be frightened.

One evening I was watching TV when I was suddenly aware that someone was standing in the dining room with me, and there she was. It was a young girl wearing a grey dress, a white pinny with white cuffs and a little white mop cap. I looked, then I turned away and thought, 'Did I see that?'. When I looked again she had gone.

The Grey Lady Gets Annoyed (Webheath)

Webheath was only a small village surrounded by farmland until the latter half of the twentieth century, when it became engulfed in new housing developments.

Jane is an attractive young lady in her mid-teens. When she was six years old she was living in Heathfield Road, Webheath. She had her own bedroom with a night-light which was kept on all night and the bedroom door was always open, so that she could see into the landing.

I used to go to sleep and then suddenly, I don't know why, I would be bolt awake. I would look across to the landing and I would see an old lady standing there, frowning and shouting at me. She never made any noise but I could see her lips moving. She was fairly tall and thin and she was wearing old-fashioned clothing. Sometimes she had her shawl over her head and at other times it would be round her shoulders. Her hair was pulled back, I think she had a bun. She was wearing a long light grey dress but it stopped just before it reached the floor and you could see through the bottom part of her so that I never saw her shoes. I can't think how I managed to see her because the landing light wasn't on and the bathroom light wouldn't have been on at that time of night, but I did see her very clearly. There wasn't any colour in her, she was all this light grey.

She used to stay there for quite a long time. I wasn't frightened, I just used to watch her and try and to make out what she was saying. The more I watched, the angrier she became. Sometimes I would shut my eyes and pull the blanket over my head, but when I looked back again she was still there. She must have been appearing once or twice a week for quite a few months.

I didn't tell my mum until after we moved house.

Jane's mother was horrified when she heard her story:

It was a real shock. We were in that house for many years and I never suspected that we had a ghost. We had a lady come once who was sensitive to that kind of thing and she said that she could feel something on the landing but I didn't take much notice. Then after we had moved, a friend of mine told me that the previous owners had seen an old lady float through the lounge. I said to her, 'You have waited all these years before you tell me'.

The Ghost on the Chat Line (Church Hill)

Church Hill housing estate was created by the Redditch Development Corporation and gets its name from Beoley Church on its northern side. In the centre was a small pool, with shops on one side and the YMCA complex with about 120 flats on two sides. The track of the old Roman road, Icknield Street, runs through the centre from north to south, while crossing it, from west to east, is a buses only lane. If a vehicle happens to arrive on the wrong side of the buses only lane it needs to make a long detour to reach the other side of the road.

Jane* lives on the southern edge of the village:

I used to live in a first floor maisonette in Abberley Close, Redditch. I was there for about seven years and during this time several strange things happened.

Often it would sound as if someone was in the other room. I would be sitting in the lounge and I would hear the noise of breaking glass coming from the kitchen, I would run out to investigate and nothing would be out of place. There were also sounds of smashing and of something falling and other noises that I couldn't quite pinpoint.

My TV sometimes switched itself on in the small hours of the morning. Also, things would move. You would put something down and a minute later it wouldn't be there and I would find it somewhere entirely different. At first, I put it down to me being absent-minded but then it all added up.

I received a telephone bill and there were quite a few calls listed on it which I hadn't made. Some of them were made in the early hours of the morning and several were made when I was on holiday at my parents' house. I queried it and BT said that they were calls made to a sex chat line. At the time, I was living on my own with a small daughter and the last thing I wanted was a chat on a sex line!

I would feel as if someone was watching me. It wasn't just me that felt it, other people would come and bring my attention to it. It wasn't an evil presence, it didn't alarm you. It never frightened me nor my daughter. We just got used to it.

My young daughter used to keep talking about this person at the end of her bed at night. It started from when she could first talk, at about eighteen months old, and went on until she was nearly eight, when we left. She said she would wake up in the night to find somebody standing at the end of her bed. She was quite matter-of-fact about it. She used to come down in the morning and say, 'He was in my room again last night'. For a long time we thought it was just an imaginary friend.

One night I had a friend to stay. She slept in the lounge and the next morning she said she was woken up by the feeling that somebody was there, and standing in the doorway was the silhouette of a man. He was there for quite a few moments before he disappeared.

I moved out five years ago, not because of the ghost but I remarried and bought a house. Nothing strange has happened in this new house and my daughter has never been visited by her friend in the night.

Mary, Mary, Quite Contrary (Rowney Green)

About 400 million years ago the Silurian Sea moved in to cover most of England and when this receded, pockets of gravel remained. One of these was at Rowney Green. Although farming was the most important occupation, gravel-working came second. The industrial activity of the gravel works has now disappeared, but the huge pits have landscaped the area.

Rita* knocked down an old cottage at Rowney Green:

We built a new house over it but, according to the law, you have to leave some footings so the base of the old house was still there. About twice a year I would see this lady there, wearing Mary, Mary Quite Contrary-type clothes. She wore this big bonnet and a beautiful dress with a nipped-in waist and a full skirt, probably early Victorian. She had two small black dogs on a taut lead. I couldn't see any colour in her, she was grey all over.

I first saw her through the kitchen window. She was in the porch and I only saw the dogs to start with because I was looking through the glass of the door. My first thought was, 'Oh, the flipping dogs have got out' because at that time I had two dogs who were very similar, but when I checked, my dogs were elsewhere.

The dining room was the original cottage. When we first moved there we had two black cats, one of them would not go into the dining room, in fact he did not like the house at all and went to live next door. We also had a big border collie and we could not get him to go into the dining room. The little black dogs were OK, perhaps because they came to us as puppies.

We lived in the house for eight years and I saw her a number of times. My family thought I was nuts.

BEOLEY

In the time of Queen Elizabeth I, Habington wrote:

> Cominge to the mannors which were purchased by the Earles of Warwicke, Beoley presenteth itself as the fyrst and worthyest, a lordship in former ages fortifyed with a Castell (Castle), the Churche mounted on a hyll in the Myddest of a large parcke replenyshed with deere, inryched (enriched) and grand with timber and woodes, and lastly the mannor attended with tenants wanting nothinge concurringe to greatenes.

Beoley Church is over 800 years old. Perhaps there was a little community of ironworkers here because the church is dedicated to Saint Leonard, their patron saint. The south and north arcade were built around 1300 and a west tower and north aisle were added only a century or two later.

Beoley Hall was occupied by the wealthy Sheldon family who developed the art of tapestry-weaving in England. Some tapestries were in the form of maps, so were both useful and decorative. In about 1600 Ralph Sheldon placed two splendid monuments in the church in memory of his father and immediate ancestors. A stone step can be pulled away from the monuments leading to the Sheldon family vaults, and the story has been told many times that, during the 1800s, a vicar decided to raise money for the church by opening up the vaults as a tourist attraction. Afterwards he was so sure that he was haunted by a ghost of the Sheldons that he paid a man to sleep at his bed at night.

The Legend of Shakespeare's Skull

There's an old legend that Beoley is associated with another famous name. The story begins one evening in the regal setting of Ragley Hall. The splendid meal was over, the ladies had retired and the men were having a quiet smoke by the soft light of the oil lamps. The conversation turned to a discussion of the bust of Shakespeare nearby. One member of the party remembered that Horace Walpole, the famous author, had offered 300 guineas (£315) for Shakespeare's skull, in those days a small fortune.

At that dinner was Dr Frank Chambers of Alcester, a man with dubious associates. Hoping to claim the 300 guineas, he hired three men to break into the tomb, Messrs Dyer, Cull and Hawtin, and arranged to pay them £3 each. One dark night they crept into Trinity Church at Stratford-on-Avon and, by the light of flickering lanterns, they prized open the tomb and took the skull. The head was that of a man with a small head and a large forehead.

Chambers wrote to Walpole saying that he had the skull, but Walpole replied that although he would like to see the skull, he had changed his mind and didn't want to buy it. Walpole offered the skull to various friends but no-one seemed interested in its purchase so he asked Dyer to return the skull to the tomb.

One December night, Dyer called on Dr Chambers in a distressed state, and asked the doctor to attend to a woman who had been taken ill in a church. The church was on a hill in an 'outlandish parish' near Redditch. The woman was a member of a team of forgers, who were living in the crypt and using lead off the coffins for their work. During the course of the evening, Dyer confessed to Dr Chambers that he had

The tower of Saint Leonard's, Beoley.

not replaced the skull. He had entered Trinity Church with the intention of doing so, but had heard someone approaching so had not finished the task. At that time it was customary to keep the bones of the deceased in a special room next to the crypt, known as the ossuary or charnel house. Dyer had wanted to get rid of the skull so had thrown it into the ossuary next to the crypt occupied by the forgers, but before doing so had broken off a sliver of bone so that he would be able to identify it if the need arose. He now handed Dr Chambers the piece of bone. Dr Chambers was never able to recover the skull, but put the bone in a small box together with an explanation.

The box fell into the hands of a Warwickshire man, who has never revealed his identity. He set about trying to locate the church. Saint Leonard's at Beoley was the most appropriate, and when he asked the verger about the ossuary, he was told about the Sheldon crypt. The verger added that there had once been an entrance to it from the churchyard but this was sealed after a group of forgers were found to be using it. The Warwickshire man sorted through the ossuary bones and there he found a small skull with a large forehead and a piece of bone missing. The sliver fitted perfectly.

No-one knows what happened to the skull. In fact, this is a tale told by suspicious characters about questionable deeds, so the whole story could be fictitious. We shall only know the truth if ever Shakespeare's body is exhumed. In the meantime, if anyone is hoarding a skull with a removable sliver of bone, could they please come forward.

Surprised in the Act!

The following story comes from a well-known character in Redditch who has threatened libel action if her name is revealed!

About eight years ago I started to 'court' a man I worked with. We both used to work the late shift at a local supermarket; I would finish work at midnight and he would finish thirty minutes later. As he lived not far from Beoley with his parents, we used to meet up after work in front of the church – I would drive there and await his arrival.

We met at the church on many occasions. We were usually too engrossed in the throes of young love and passion to be very aware of our surroundings. Until one night, when we heard a strange noise, felt that we were being watched but couldn't see anything at all, and went very, very cold. I don't know what was there but it spooked us both badly, so badly in fact that I drove away at high speed – stark naked! Can you imagine it!

We are both calm and rational people, not prone to being jumpy at all but we both felt a presence of something unpleasant. We never returned there at night again and I still get goosebumps when I drive past the church at night. Anyway, we are happily married now.

Flowers for Remembrance Sunday

Anyone who has visited Beoley Church will be full of admiration for the flower arrangements by church members. These patient ladies create works of art that wither away after a week or two. Heather Hill is one of them:

My hobby is flower arranging and in November 1982, I was very honoured to be asked to arrange the flowers at Beoley Church for Remembrance Sunday. I was chosen because my daughter is in the navy. I managed to get hold of a soldier's helmet and I surrounded it with flowers and autumn leaves – oak, beech, copper beech and so on.

I got very involved, I worked until late at night and it gave me a splitting migraine. I had hoped to go to the Remembrance Sunday service but I didn't know if I could make it. Later that night, my daughter phoned and invited my husband and myself down to Portsmouth where she would be on parade, but I said that I couldn't go, I felt too drained.

At about three o'clock on the Sunday morning I woke up thinking, 'I feel better today'. I couldn't get back to sleep, I lay there for an hour until the day was breaking. Then I thought, 'What's happening?'. In the corner of the room was a small statue of a soldier wearing the helmet. I wasn't asleep, I am sure. The statue grew bigger and bigger, he was the colour of sandstone and so was the background but he stood out clearly. He came nearer and nearer, just looking at me, then when he got quite close he suddenly smiled. I saw his features so clearly that if I was shown his photograph, I would recognise him. I dropped off to sleep and never thought any more about it, but put it down to the fact that I had been concentrating too much on my flower arranging.

I felt fine the next morning and I said to my husband, 'Come on, we're going to Portsmouth'. I was so glad I went, we knew my daughter would be on parade but we didn't know she would be leading it.

We were so proud. We also met my future son-in-law for the first time. The amazing thing was, that there, etched on the gate or wall of Portsmouth barracks, was the soldier in my dream. He was there just as I had seen him, the colour of sandstone, standing out from the background, and wearing the same type of helmet that I had borrowed. It wasn't something which had lain dormant in my memory, this was the first time I had seen the carving.

Head from Beoley font circa 1140.

STUDLEY (WARWICKSHIRE)

 tudley claims to be the largest village in England. The Roman Ryknield Street passes through the centre and by 1200 it had a church, a priory and a castle. The church is still there, mostly rebuilt, the priory has disappeared and although Studley now has a castle, this is half a mile away from the site of the old one and was built in 1833.

Redditch is famous for the manufacture of needles but, in actual fact, the first record of needle-making in the area is at Studley when a William Lea settled there from London during the second quarter of the 17th century. In the twentieth century it was the home of the Needle Industries, which, at its peak, employed about 1,500 people. The company has now been renamed Entaco Limited and still produces about ten million hand-sewing needles each week.

The Bank Manager and the Flying Gateau

A narrow road known as Marble Alley runs behind the Co-op in the centre of Studley and on its far side was a row of small shops which have now mostly been converted to houses. They were probably built in the early years of Queen Victoria's reign as cottages for needle workers but have now been enlarged and modernised. In 1996 Jean Sealey took over one of these premises which had been empty for five years and, with a great deal of hard work, converted it into a cheese shop and delicatessen, specialising in local cheeses. 'Bon Appetit' was so successful that a year later she was able to turn the upstairs into a cafeteria.

> When we first opened up all kinds of strange little things happened but we didn't think anything about them. Lots of things kept falling off the shelves for no reason. We used to hear noises upstairs, sometimes it would sound as if somebody was walking across the floorboards and there hadn't been anybody up there for years. We have heard people go up and down the stairs and gone out to look but nobody is there. I used to think it was just the floorboards creaking. I'm not the only one who heard the noises, several times the two girls who were working here remarked on them.

The shops in Marble Alley, Studley (now converted to houses).

After a few months we started doing a lot of alterations upstairs. We pulled up the carpets, knocked down a wall to make it into one big room, turned a bedroom into a kitchen and put in a new toilet. The strange things got much worse after that. We seemed to have disturbed something. Just before we opened we could hear the new toilet flushing and the water running in the pipes when no-one was up there.

Then, just after we opened, there was this flood in the upstairs kitchen. A sixteen-year old Saturday girl came rushing down to say that they had a flood in the kitchen upstairs. The water was gushing out of an outside wall but we couldn't find where it was coming from and the strange thing was that there were no pipes in that area. We never discovered the source and eventually it stopped just as mysteriously as it had started. It has never happened since although we do tend to get mysterious puddles. The floorboards are uneven and we get puddles wherever the floorboards dip. Again, there's often no water supply anywhere near the puddle.

I have seen things moving. We have three boxes, about ten centimetres square, on top of one of the shelves downstairs and I have seen those moving quite quickly from side to side and backwards and forwards. I tell myself that it's probably a draft so I shut the doors and switch the fan off but they still move. We had a delivery man here once and he was just standing there, at the counter, when one of the boxes flew off and just glanced his shoulder.

We have had problems with flying cakes. I particularly remember one day when the Bank Manager was here. We were upstairs, sorting out some details, and I had made him a cup of coffee. I went to take it over to him and a large carrot cake sitting on the top of a plastic cake container flew a distance of about four feet. He looked at me and I looked at him. He said, 'What made it do that?' I told him that we had a ghost. He didn't make any comment and just carried on with what he was doing but he never came back!

I have had a problem with the freezer. I know that I shut the freezer door before I went home but when I came back on the Saturday morning it was open and everything was defrosted. I said to my assistant, 'Just get rid of the stuff and give the freezer a good clean'. We did this and we still couldn't shut the door. There was no reason for it, it wasn't catching on anything and nothing had warped. It felt as if someone was pushing the door open from the inside. I said, 'We'll leave it, perhaps it got too hot or it's something to do with the electricity supply' so we left it for two or three days but we still couldn't shut it. I called out a refrigeration engineer but he couldn't find anything wrong and he said that I might have to have a new freezer. I came in towards the end of the next week and as I walked past, I slammed it shut and it closed! We haven't had any trouble since. The strange thing is, I had been thinking that I must get round to defrosting the freezer and it had done itself for me. Sometimes these strange happenings seem linked to what I have been thinking.

Occasionally, I would come in first thing in the morning and I would find a child's handprints all over the glass refrigeration counter upstairs. I would know that I had cleaned it thoroughly just before I went home at night. We also had a large dish of tea leaves on the counter and sometimes I would find indentations in it, as if a child had dipped his or her finger in it and dragged it along. I would know that no children had come into the cafeteria and it wasn't the sort of thing an adult would do. I wasn't surprised, therefore, when a lady came into the shop who said that she was psychic and she felt that we had the ghost of a child here. I wondered why it had chosen the carrot cake to throw. Perhaps it didn't like carrot cake.

I have never had anything like this happen in any other premises but the ghost doesn't bother me. There's no harm in any of these incidents, nobody gets hurt and they seem to be just mischievous. It's a nice atmosphere here. Fortunately the lady who helps me is very interested in that sort of thing so she doesn't mind it at all. I've been working here at midnight and I've never felt frightened or threatened. Mostly, it's just amusing but it can be annoying when I have to mop up puddles or throw away the freezer contents or put a perfectly good carrot cake in the bin.

Religious Laxities (The Barley Mow)

Right in the centre of Studley, across the road from the Barley Mow and behind the garage, was an Augustinian priory, founded in the 12th century. The Studley historian, Dr Ray Shaw, says that if the priory accounts are accurate then it seems that the monks were far more likely to be flat on their backs in the brew-house than on their knees in the Church.

In 1319, the priory was described as 'a riotous house' and in 1364, a visiting Prior of Worcester was met by 'bows and weapons' when he came to admonish the monks for 'religious laxity'.

A collection of ghost stories about the Barley Mow was published in *Haunted Pubs and Hotels of Worcestershire and its Borders*. Mary and Arthur Payton saw the book and Mary has contributed the following.

The Barley Mow, Studley.

Arthur was the licensee of the Barley Mow from 1962 to 1968. When we went there Mitchells and Butlers had just bought it from Thompsons Brewery of Studley and it was real old place. In medieval times it had been a store house for the Priory across the road and then it used to be a hostelry for people travelling along the old Salt Road from Droitwich to Birmingham which went past its doors. There were genuine oak beams everywhere with the old joint holes, and some of them looked like old ship's timbers to me. The Crown used to own the rights on old timbers and when a ship was demolished builders used to buy these timbers, as after a few years at sea they were really hard, you couldn't even knock nails in. One of them was 27 inches thick, now that's some beam. There was a section at the side which was part of an ancient brewery and there was even a priest hole up-stairs. The place was badly lit and a bit eerie.

We had a large number of staff who stayed with us for a long time. We were a sociable crowd and at the end of each evening we would sit round and have a drink. That was in the time when you closed at ten o'clock. Sometimes, five or six of us would be sitting there and we would notice that all of a sudden, everyone would stop talking and we would all look at the same point. We had not seen anything but everybody was aware of something in the room. Those who were sitting with their back to it would turn round. You didn't feel it coming in but you knew it was there. We were convinced it was a monk and we named him 'Charlie'.

It was never frightening, it was just like a friend who had come in. I was often alone when Arthur was called away as a Relief Manager to another pub, and I never felt afraid.

In those days there was a bar, then a counter, and behind these a short passage. We were grouped round one evening after we had closed, I was standing with my back to the fireplace and facing the passageway when I suddenly stopped talking and said, 'Someone has just gone along that passage'. I can see him in my mind's eye now. He was tall and grey with a cowl. I thought at first it was the shadow of a bus going past, but the more I thought about it the more I could see that this was impossible.

This passageway had various doors leading from it, one went to the cellars, another to our living quarters and yet another to a little room at the back which we had made into a cigarette and spirits store. We had acquired a Boxer dog and obviously, the best place to keep a big dog from the point of view of security was in the passageway, between the stores and the cellar. But would he go in there? I literally had to pick him up and force him in there. He would shake and wet himself with fright. Unfortunately we had to get rid of him in the end as he was turning into a nervous wreck.

Then there were the latches. After you have been managing a pub for a short while you get into a routine and Arthur used to lock up in sequence, working his way round to the bar. You are very careful about locking up because of the security aspect. We would finish locking up and go into our own quarters when all of a sudden we would hear a click and that door would be open. They were the old-fashioned heavy iron latches and solid oak doors and no way could they lift themselves and the doors swing open of their own accord. All this happened just in the area of the bar and the passageway.

Other members of staff had strange experiences – we had a barman named Benny who was a real tough character, frightened of neither man nor beast, and many times I have seen him go into the kitchen for ice and come back with his hair standing on end.

Mitchells and Butlers carried out extensive alterations to the Barley Mow. The upstairs was hung on girders while they rebuilt the whole of downstairs. The alterations took fourteen months. After that we never felt or witnessed anything again.

Aunty Says 'Goodbye'

Josie* lives near the centre of the village. She and her husband were very fond of her husband's aunty who was 98 years old and lived in London:

We often used to go and see her and take our little dog, Ben*, with us. The last couple of times we went we didn't take the dog and she was very disappointed.

I was in bed one morning and my husband was up the garden when I heard the dog barking and growling. I didn't bother to get up and see what the matter was as my husband was on his way back down the garden. Our kitchen leads into the dining room so that he could see across the dining table. Ben stood there facing the outside window, he was looking at something and his tail was wagging. My husband looked to see what Ben was looking at and there was his aunty. She was wearing a dress and smiling, just in black and white, looking as if she had walked out of a black and white television. She had a kind of aura around her. As he looked she just faded away. She died soon afterwards.

We thought perhaps she had come to say goodbye to Ben.

Never Without Some Ghost or Other

A hundred and fifty years ago, Tom's Town in Studley was said to be 'never without some ghost or other'. A stone's throw from Tom's Town is New Road, also a rich source of ghost stories through the years. This one dates back to the early 1940s and is told by Pep, one of Dudley's Coaches (in Radford) most popular coach drivers:

When my mother was about fourteen or fifteen she lived in New Road and at one time she was in bed and quite ill. She may have had a temperature or something. During the night she woke up. At first, she didn't know whether she was dreaming or not, but it soon became apparent that whatever she heard was real. She could hear footsteps coming up the stairs, very heavy, one at a time, and with them a laboured breathing. On the landing, one bedroom went off to the left and another to the right, hers was on the left. She heard these footsteps turn to the left and come into her bedroom. She was lying on her back and she closed her eyes tightly. The footsteps came over to her bed and she not only heard the breathing but she could feel the breath on her face. Then the footsteps went back three steps and stopped.

The next morning she asked if anyone had been into her room at night but nobody had. She told them what had happened and the family laughed it off, they said she must have been delirious or something. It passed over.

However, they had an old sheepdog and every now and then the dog looked as if she had been frightened to death. All her hairs would stand up on end.

All the children got married and went their separate ways, but her brother, my uncle, came back to live in the same house. He and his wife were sleeping in that same bedroom for twenty years and never heard anything strange. Nothing was ever mentioned. Whatever it was seemed to have gone completely.

Then they were lying in bed one night and my uncle heard the laboured footsteps and the heavy breathing coming up the stairs. The footsteps came into his room. He lay there, listening, then he jumped out of bed and said, 'There's someone else in this bedroom besides you and me'. Unknown to him, my aunty was already awake and she had been lying in bed listening to the footsteps as well. So they both heard them.

During the 1960s I moved into the house. I lived there for years and years and never heard anything, but one of the neighbours did tell me that, many years before, the man in the house next door had hung himself and I did wonder if that was anything to do with it.

An Old-Fashioned Curse

It's not very often these days that you come across a good old-fashioned curse. At one time, every witch had a nasty curse at her fingertips. Even men of the cloth did their best to summon damnation for unpopular individuals. When Saint Egwin preached to the men of Bromsgrove they made such a clatter with their anvils that he could not be heard, and so, when he left, he shook off the dust from his sandals and cursed the town.

At Worcester, the Norman sheriff, Urse d'Abitot, widened the defences of Worcester castle and encroached on the monks burying ground. Bishop Wulstan sent for the Archbishop, who examined the ground then cursed the sheriff to his face, saying:

Highest thou Urse

Have thou God's curse.

The Chroniclers say that the curse was so effective that the sheriff's son died young and the family line died out.

As recently as 1963, Reverend Ernest Street, rector of a church in Bramber, Sussex, cursed those who had left black mass symbols around his churchyard and desecrated the graves. In the rite of exorcism known as Bell, Book and Candle, a curse is read from a book which is then slammed shut. Even today, there are people who believe they have been cursed. The recommended course of action is to find someone who is an expert in the paranormal to remove the curse.

The following story was told at a meeting in Studley Village Hall:

At the other end of Crooks Lane to the swimming baths used to be a pub, called the Grove. One of the roads is called after it. I think it was owned by a Mr Crooks, that's where Crooks Lane comes from.

Worcestershire Ghosts and Hauntings

This pub was converted into an old cottage and a little old lady lived there, we used to call her Ducky. She was able to cast spells on people. One of our neighbours used to pop in and see her husband whenever she was out. Ducky asked us to keep an eye on her because she thought she was having it off with her husband. Well, we knew she was but we didn't say anything. One day she caught them at it. She said to us afterwards, 'I have put a spell on her'. Anyway, this other woman developed something wrong with her leg and from that day onwards she was never able to work.

When Ducky knew that her cottage was to be demolished and houses built on the site she told us, 'They'll never do any good, I've put a spell on them'. Well, do you know, two builders went bankrupt and another had to undo all his work because the footings were wrong.

There's a Man in My Bedroom

Recently demolished the building which was The Griffin Public House was once a needle factory and was twice its present size. It stretched back along Green Lane. A Studley businessman who died in 1996 used to talk about one evening in 1925, when he was a young lad of fourteen, and went to visit relatives in Redditch. It was a brilliant moonlit night and he was just going past The Griffin when he saw a huge black stage coach and horses advancing rapidly towards him. He fell off his

The Griffin Inn, Green Lane, Studley (now demolished).

bike in fright. As the coach neared him it disappeared. He never dared cycle that way again.

Melinda, who works in Colorama in the Redditch shopping centre, can tell you all about the ghost of Green Lane:

When I was about nineteen, I lived with my friend Linda in an old house in Green Lane, Studley, by The Griffin. She was about the same age, we were at college together. Her parents had divorced and gone their separate ways and left her the house to live in.

Late one evening I went to bed and first of all I decided to read. I switched the overlight on but found that I didn't feel like reading so I closed my book and switched the light off. Straight away I felt that there was somebody in the room. My first thought was that Linda, who had gone out, had come back but then I looked across the room and there, standing in the corner, about ten feet away, was a chap. I can see him to this day. He was bald, with a little bit of hair round the side, and he wore glasses. He was only small, about 5 feet 5 inches and plump, with a belly on him. He had on a knitted baggy green waistcoat and baggy trousers in a plain dark grey. His shirt was a very pale check, it looked worn out. He seemed to be worried and was rubbing his fingers together, it seemed as if he was looking for something.

I sat bolt upright in bed. I was terrified, you don't expect to see that sort of thing, do you? He was there for quite a few seconds, perhaps a minute or two, then I blinked and he was gone.

When Linda came home she told me that her mother had also seen the ghost. Her mother thought it must be the person who used to live there twenty or so years ago, his wife had passed away and she thought he came back looking for her.

WORCESTERSHIRE – GENERAL

The Dental Surgeon and the Choir Boy

A dental surgeon who lives and works in Worcestershire has a beautiful old cottage in a wooded area. It was once three workers' cottages and he has spent years converting them into a family home. He now lives there with his wife, Vivienne* and their extended family. Vivienne opens the conversation:

> None of our rebuilding has been that drastic. We have tried to keep the building pretty much as it was originally. The most ambitious thing we have done is to knock down a wall between two rooms and make them into one. Nevertheless we seem to have problems here whenever we have done some rebuilding.
>
> We have the odd thing happen. Sometimes the lights come on of their own accord. Our cat was fast asleep on my bed one night when suddenly, all the stair lights came on, the four side lights and the main light. The cat shot off the bed. Another time we were having a party here when the lights on the stairs suddenly came on. The strange thing is that all our light switches click but when the lights come on of their own accord there is no clicking noise.
>
> I came back from shopping one day to find the kitchen tap running full blast. Our taps are the kind that you

need to lift up to operate so it is unlikely that I would inadvertently leave a tap running.

One or two things have a strange habit of disappearing, I have a small brush which I use to brush the pile on the three piece suite. I know that I had it in the lounge but that disappeared about two months ago and I haven't seen it since.

We lived in a mess for a very long time, we had no carpets – just bare floorboards – and furniture scattered here and there. In our bedroom was an old dressing table. At that time I had three dogs and they wandered all over the house. One evening, we had gone to bed and we must have been asleep when I was woken up by a bark from one of the dogs who slept in a basket in our bedroom. Kneeling down at the dressing table was a choir boy. He had blond hair with a side parting, and he was wearing a red and white chorister's gown. He looked very real. I watched him for a while until he faded.

I happened to mention this to my husband on the Sunday morning and he immediately collared two of the old locals and asked them if they knew anything about it. They recognised the apparition as a young man who had lived in the middle cottage and who had been killed in action during the war.

My parents-in-law sometimes come to stay and they have the bedroom next to ours. There are interconnecting doors between each bedroom. My mother-in-law told us that she woke up in the night to see someone come from the door leading into our bedroom, carrying something like a baby or a bible. Then he turned and went out onto the landing. At first my mother thought it was my father but when she looked at my father's bed he was fast asleep.

The local vicar was a lovely person so I asked him to call. I told him what had been going on and I said that I just wanted some advice. He was a great believer in things like this after a strange experience during the war. He said that the spirit didn't want to hurt us and that we should talk to it. He told us not to be frightened and that we should leave the Bible open at a certain page. He said he would be bringing a party of people in to bless the house but I didn't fancy that, I didn't want to have a lot of strange people tramping through my house.

My husband knew a paranormal expert and she came over. She said that the spirit didn't mean to cause us any harm. After she had been it all went quiet.

Vivienne's husband had been sitting listening, but he now took up the story:

> We had been living here for some years and I hadn't seen anything peculiar except for one minor incident some years ago when I was coming home, and from across the road I thought I saw somebody move across one of the upstairs windows. I had the impression that it was a male. I came in and said to my wife, 'Who's upstairs?' and she said, 'Nobody'. Thinking that somebody had broken in I shot upstairs but nobody was there.
>
> We have a square landing with a door at the far side which leads into the end bedroom. I was working with the base of a bed and a large reel of underfelt; I had finished the floor area inside the door, but when I opened the door to do the outside I saw a man standing there. He was tall and slim, perhaps approaching sixty. I noticed that he was wearing a very narrow tie with the tiepin on the underside of the knot, and his hair was greased down close to his head. He was very solid, his body blocked out the light so that I couldn't see the bed and the underfelt. I was so surprised that I didn't speak to him. Then he disappeared and I remember thinking, 'I can see the bed and the underfelt now'.

Both Vivienne and her husband agreed that they didn't mind their strange residents but they would like to know more about them – who they were, what they were and why they should make themselves known.

Extracting the Ghost

In Edgbaston is a dental surgery where all kinds of strange things have taken place. During a little celebration one day, the dentist was standing with a gin and tonic in his hand when it was snatched away. On another occasion, he was knocked down the stairs, he said later it felt as if he had someone's knee in his back. He could not get up. Another time he was held back by an invisible force. He called out a paranormal expert who told him that he was being haunted by a lady with four daughters who had previously lived in the premises. The lady objected to him being there.

Another haunted surgery exists in Worcestershire. The dental surgeon concerned was very reluctant to tell his story and minor amendments have been made to preserve anonymity:

I bought this old Victorian house about ten years ago and converted it into a dental surgery, with facilities on the first floor and on the ground floor. Over the first eight years or so we had one or two strange incidents. A door upstairs occasionally locked itself from the inside of the room. This shouldn't be possible. We had to get the door off its hinges to get into the room.

We had an old bathroom upstairs and I got there one morning to find the hot tap full on. Nobody would own up to having left it running.

My colleague was working upstairs when some invisible force knocked him on the head. He had a nurse with him and she saw his head go right back. He was OK but quite shocked.

Late one evening around Christmas time I had told everyone to go home except for a nurse downstairs. I was upstairs, clearing up, when the nurse ran up the stairs and asked me what the matter was. She said that she had heard a scream. I told her that I hadn't screamed. She stopped upstairs and I went down and what should I hear but a scream upstairs. I ran up, thinking she had been attacked or something but she hadn't screamed.

That was all that happened until we had some major alterations done and then all hell was let loose. The upstairs door has been locked from the inside loads of times and there's no way you can lock that door from the inside. The hot tap has been repeatedly turned on overnight.

Nurses and other members of staff have been pushed, poked or knocked, they have all had something happen to them. Some of them now refuse to go upstairs.

The burglar alarm went off at one o'clock in the morning. It's a very sophisticated alarm and had detected a movement around the bathroom area. I couldn't turn the damn thing off. I called the police out and I told the constable, 'I know it's two o'clock in the morning and this sounds unbelievable but a lot of strange things have been happening here lately'. He said, 'I'm not surprised, a lot of strange things have been happening in the road'.

All the control panels had blown out, the security guys who came out to repair it said that they had never seen that before. What had happened, was that at one o'clock in the morning there had been a total power drop and this had set off the alarms in that area. About half an hour later the drop had been reassessed as a power surge and that's when I opened the door. In other words I had disturbed something when I opened the door. We had to have new control panels.

The couple who lived in the house before I had bought it happened to register with me as patients. I didn't want to be sensationalist, so I said to them, quite casually, 'Did you have any problems while you were here?'. They said, 'Yes, we had a ghost'. Something or other had been happening to them all the time. Pictures had dropped off the wall in the corridor and objects had been flying around. Bath taps kept turning themselves full on. Their son reckoned that a black figure came out of the wall and fell on top of him in bed. They said it went quiet for a year before they left.

We don't tell anyone about the ghost because it would be bad for business. However, an elderly lady, who is a patient of ours, came to us straight from a clairvoyant meeting. At that meeting, the medium claimed to have contacted a spirit from our dental surgery (she named the surgery) which said that it didn't like what was being done to its home. The living accommodation had been turned into a commercial venture.

I was worried because some people felt that they were being pushed. What would happen if someone was pushed down steps here and there upstairs, or even down a flight of stairs? I decided to have the place exorcised and called in a paranormal specialist. As soon as he walked upstairs he felt a 'being' round the landing and bathroom area. He said it was not a nice spirit. We haven't had any problems since he came.

Removing a bad tooth in the eighteenth century.
Dentists were unknown and the work was usually
carried out by the local barber.

EPILOGUE

Many of the stories in this book go back some years. There are probably just as many hauntings now as there were some ten, twenty or thirty years ago, but people are reluctant to talk about them. It is only when some years have passed that they come into the open. Many of the contributors in this book who tell of recent events found that doing so was very painful and we are very grateful to them for putting aside their emotions and telling us about their experiences.

One of Worcestershire's leading churchmen performs many blessings (some would say exorcisms) each year and he writes:

> Most of the people we speak to are frightened, sometimes terrified, at what is going on around them and need confidentiality and gentle pastoral care. The last thing they would want is to see details of their particular situation in the printed word.
>
> Yes, we do use bell, book and candle and never publicise it and back off if there is any hint of publicity and as such feel that many of us have had success. The procedure is quite simple; a bowl of salt water is blessed, the sign of the cross is made on the door post of each door with prayer and we pray for the peace of the distressed spirit and that is all.
>
> What little I have given, you may use anonymously.

*The Malvern Hills, where the
Witch of Eldersfield once lived.*

BIBLIOGRAPHY

Belling's Directory and Gazetteer of the County of Worcester, 1855.

Brassington, Historic Worcestershire, 1894, Midland Educational Company Limited.

Brown W Alfred, *Evesham Friends in Olden Times*, 1885, no publisher but printer was West, Newman & Co. (In Evesham library).

Cullum WCI, *A History of Studley and the Surrounding Area*, 1980, published privately.

Fraser Maxwell, *Companion into Worcestershire*, 1939, Methuen.

Gwilliam HG, *Old Worcester*, Volume One, 1977 Rose Hill House Teachers' Centre.

Haughton Brian, *Coaching Days in the Midlands*, 1997 Quercus.

Nash Treadway Dr, *History of Worcestershire*, second edition, 1799.

Neville Havins Peter J, *Portrait of Worcestershire*, 1974 Robert Hale, London,

Noake John, *The Rambler*, MDCCCLL, Longman & Co.

Palmer Roy, *The Folklore of Hereford and Worcester*, 1992, Logaston Press,

Pevsner Niklaus, *The Buildings of England, Worcestershire*, 1968 Penguin.

Richards Alan and others, *Bygone Bromsgrove*, 1981 The Bromsgrove Society, also excerpts from *'The Rousler'* published by the Bromsgrove Society.

Symonds WS, *Malvern Chase*, 1913 William North and Simpkin, Marshall, Hamilton, Kent & Co Ltd.

Victoria County History (The), *A History of the County of Worcestershire*, published for the University of London Institute of Historical Research, 1913.

Watson Bruce, *Offenham Village and Maypole: An Illustrated Guide*, Sponsored by Offenham Wake Committee, 2001, sold by Evesham Almonry at £1.30.

Willis Bund JW *The Civil War in Worcestershire 1642-1646*, 1979 Alan Sutton Publishing Ltd.

Worcestershire Village Book (The), 1988, Worcestershire Federation of Women's Institutes.

Also other pamphlets, booklets etc too numerous to mention.

The *William Avery Memorial Papers* are in Redditch library and were collected between 1823 and William Avery's death in 1899. His friend, William Page, worked on the arrangement of the collection until 1906. The ghost stories are from volume 1 and are cuttings from the *Redditch Indicator*.

An asterisk after a name means that a pseudonym has been used.

Books by Anne Bradford

True Life Ghost Stories
Ghosts, Murders and Scandals I £9.95.
Ghosts, Murders and Scandals II £9.95.
Worcestershire the Haunted County £9.95.
Worcestershire Ghosts and Hauntings £9.95.
The Haunted Midlands £9.95.
Haunted Pubs of Worcestershire £7.50.
Foul Deeds and Suspicious Deaths around Worcestershire £10.99.

Oral History Books
Royal Enfield, the company and the people who made it great £14.95.
Stourport-on-Severn, a history of the town and the area £11.95.
My family and other misfits (an autobiography) £7.00.
Old Redditch being an early history of the town written by
Mr Avery between 1800 and 1850, edited by Anne Bradford £6.95.

Books by John Bradford

Severn's Southern Hills £12.95.
Shropshire's Border Hills £12.95.
The River Teme £14.95.
The River Severn £14.95.